Naoual Nassiri

Evaluation of Arabic language readability

Naoual Nassiri

Evaluation of Arabic language readability

ScienciaScripts

Imprint
Any brand names and product names mentioned in this book are subject to trademark, brand or patent protection and are trademarks or registered trademarks of their respective holders. The use of brand names, product names, common names, trade names, product descriptions etc. even without a particular marking in this work is in no way to be construed to mean that such names may be regarded as unrestricted in respect of trademark and brand protection legislation and could thus be used by anyone.

Cover image: www.ingimage.com

This book is a translation from the original published under ISBN 978-620-6-70004-3.

Publisher:
Sciencia Scripts
is a trademark of
Dodo Books Indian Ocean Ltd. and OmniScriptum S.R.L publishing group

120 High Road, East Finchley, London, N2 9ED, United Kingdom
Str. Armeneasca 28/1, office 1, Chisinau MD-2012, Republic of Moldova, Europe
Printed at: see last page
ISBN: 978-620-8-29597-4

Contents

Acknowledgements

First of all, I would like to thank Allah for giving me the health, ability and opportunity to undertake this research study and to carry it out satisfactorily.

This thesis would not have seen the light of day without the enormous and endless support, advice and encouragement of my thesis supervisor, Professor ***Abdelhak Lakhouaja***, for whom my thanks are also insufficient. I would like to take this opportunity to express my gratitude to Mrs ***Violetta Caval li-Sforza***, who improved this thesis with her advice, support, encouragement and participation as co-director of this research work. I thank her sincerely.

I would like to thank Professors ***Arsalane Zarghili***, ***Azzeddine Mazroui*** and ***Hammou Fadili*** for agreeing to report on this thesis despite their busy schedules. My sincere thanks go to Professor ***Abdelouafi Meziane*** for agreeing to chair my thesis jury, and to Professor ***El Wardani Dadi*** for doing me the honour of being a member.

I would like to thank my friends in the LaRI laboratory. Each of them has contributed to make my stay in this PhD programme more fun and interesting. Furthermore, having ***Safae Berrichi*** as my colleague, best friend and second sibling is a great privilege and joy, and I would like to thank her for believing in me and my goals and for always supporting me.

Finally, I dedicate this thesis to my two brothers and my sister ***Safae***, who has always supported me. Without your love, care and patience, I could not have achieved this. The special dedication of this thesis is addressed to the dearest of mothers and the dearest of fathers. Thank you for your patience, your care and everything you have done to bring our family together in peace and happiness. Thank you for giving us the love we need to survive in this life. A big thank you to all the ***Nassiri*** family and the ***Oujidi*** family for their support.

Resume

Readability, represented by the complexity of vocabulary and syntax, plays an important role in the process of choosing materials adapted to the levels of pupils and readers. In fact, the task of automatically measuring the level of difficulty of a text frequently comes up against challenges such as the lack of data and resources needed to develop such systems.

In this thesis, we have produced a set of automatic readability prediction models. These models are intended for readers of Arabic as a first language (L1) and as a second or foreign language (L2). The development of these models involves three main stages. The first step consists in collecting a reference corpus annotated according to levels of difficulty. To this end, we have collected and developed four corpora, three of which are intended for L2 and the fourth for L1. The second stage of the process consists of converting the texts into feature vectors. During this second stage, the most important task is the identification of the set of characteristics that best predict the readability level of a given text. The extraction of these features is based on morphological information, extracted using morphological analysers, and on frequency information, extracted from a frequency dictionary that we have developed in the course of this research. The final stage in the development of a predictive readability model is a classification phase. For this last stage, we used four different algorithms.

In the last part of this thesis, we have exploited all the resources and models we have developed for an initial investigation into the field of text simplification. Text simplification consists of transforming a text to make it easy to understand.

Keywords : Legibility; Arabic language; TALN; L1; L2; Simplification; Education.

ملخص

تلعب المقروئية، التي تتمثل في صعوبة المفردات والنحو، دورًا مهمًا في عملية تزويد الطلاب والقراء بنصوص ذات صعوبة مناسبة. غالبًا ما تواجه مهمة القياس الآلي لمستوى صعوبة النص تحديات مثل نقص البيانات والموارد اللازمة لتطوير مثل هذه الأنظمة.

في إطار هذه الأطروحة، قمنا بإنتاج مجموعة من نماذج الحساب الآلي لقابلية القراءة. هذه النماذج مخصصة لقراء اللغة العربية كلغة أولى وكلغة ثانية أو لغة أجنبية. يمر تطوير هذه النماذج بثلاث مراحل رئيسية. تتمثل الخطوة الأولى في جمع ذخيرة لغوية موسمة بمستويات الصعوبة. من أجل ذلك قمنا بتجميع وتطوير أربع ذخائر، ثلاثة منها مخصصة للغة العربية كلغة أجنبية والرابعة مخصصة للغة العربية كلغة أولى. تتمثل الخطوة الثانية في تحويل النصوص إلى متجهات الخصائص. خلال هذه الخطوة الثانية، تتمثل المهمة الأكثر أهمية في تحديد مجموعة الخصائص التي تمكننا من تحديد مستوى صعوبة نص معين بشكل أفضل. يعتمد استخراج هذه الخصائص على المعلومات الصرفية، المستخرجة باستخدام محلل صرفي، وعلى نسب التكرار المستخرجة من قاموس التكرار الذي قمنا بتطويره خلال هذه الأطروحة. الخطوة الأخيرة في تطوير مثل هذه النماذج هي مرحلة التصنيف. لإنجاز هذه الخطوة الأخيرة، استخدمنا أربع خوارزميات مختلفة.

في الجزء الأخير من هذه الأطروحة، قمنا باستعمال الموارد والنماذج التي طورناها في محاولة أولى من أجل تبسيط النصوص. حيث يتمثل تبسيط النص في تحويل نص صعب قصد تسهيل فهمه.

كلمات مفتاحية : المقروئية؛ اللغة العربية؛ المعالجة الآلية للغات الطبيعية؛ لغة أولى؛ لغة أجنبية؛ تبسيط؛ التعليم.

General introduction

Apergu general

Clearly, reading is not a natural skill; it is a whole learning process that requires the use of an adapted teaching programme. Readers have the right to read texts adapted to their ability; by negotiating texts well beyond their level of competence, they may lose the general meaning of the text when confronted with difficult or unfamiliar vocabulary elements or constructions. In general, the easier a text is to read and the clearer the ideas it contains, the more likely it is to attract and hold the reader's attention. It is therefore useful to measure the readability of a text in terms of its clarity and ease of comprehension.

[Al-Khalifa and Al-Ajlan, 2010] have stated that "readability depends on three main factors: the reader, the text and the situation". Readability is a measure that relates a written text to a reader or grade level. It is affected by the reader's ability to understand a text and is therefore a crucial indicator in determining the target population for a given text, which has an impact on the education of pupils on the one hand and the general public (e.g. newspaper readers) on the other. Readability can play an important role in many areas in addition to education, for example in the dissemination of health information.

Legibility depends on both the content of a text and its presentation. It can be influenced by the visual appearance of the text, which refers to features such as the font in which the text is written, the colours used, the sharpness of the image, and other such visual features. [Gray and Leary, 1935] conducted a study in which they asked groups of librarians, editors and teachers what they thought made a book readable. To a reader, a book is readable if :

1. The content or subject is interesting and attractive;
2. The style of expression is comprehensible and interesting;
3. The format and organisation make it easy to follow the logic of the teaching material with a minimum of effort.

The difference between the two families of legibility (linguistic and visual) can be summed up in the fact that visual legibility depends on :

- Environmental conditions or interferences, such as lighting or vibrations, which affect the human visual system [Mustonen et al., 2004];
- The observation distance (i.e. the angular size of the symbols);
- Police design [SMITH, 1979];
- The quality of the reproduction (for example, sufficient contrast in brightness between the symbols and their background).

Whereas the second family of legibility (linguistic legibility) depends more on the language, the vocabulary used, sentence structure, etc., than on the language itself. In this thesis, we focus on linguistic readability.

Challenge

The first basic requirement for the development of a powerful readability prediction system is the reference corpus. For languages in which the reading process has been the subject of in-depth research, standard reference corpora have been collected, such as the Contemporary American English[1] corpus or the Cambridge English[2] corpus. For Arabic, there is a great lack of educational corpora dedicated to readability.

Once the reference corpus has been assembled, the second challenge encountered in developing

---

1 `https://www.english-corpora.org/coca/` (last visited on 06/11/2020)

2 `https://www.cambridge.es/en/about-us/cambridge-english-corpus` (last visited on 06/11/2020)

these tools and models is to identify a set of linguistic characteristics, also known as predictors. These must have a significant correlation with the difficulty of the texts. However, a good predictor must fulfil a number of conditions, in particular, it must correlate as little as possible with other predictors to avoid information redundancy. These characteristics will serve as input vectors for the classification algorithms later in the process. The choice of classification algorithm to be used is another challenge to be addressed when developing readability prediction models.
Finally, the development of these models can only be achieved with the help of a set of tools and resources, i.e. analysers, frequency dictionaries, lexicons, etc. Once again, the quality of these analysers and resources is a challenge to be overcome in order to increase the quality of readability prediction models. Once again, the quality of these analysers and resources is a challenge to be overcome in order to increase the quality of readability prediction models.

Objectives

The main objective of this thesis is to demonstrate the measurement of the readability of Arabic texts, particularly educational texts. Furthermore, we wish to contribute to the enrichment of resources that support the development of readability prediction systems for the Arabic language. This is mainly about :

- The development and collection of corpora for assessing the readability of texts intended for learners of Arabic as a mother tongue (L1) and as a first foreign language (L2);
- The development of a frequency dictionary for the Arabic language to support the development of prediction models;
- The collection, adaptation and development of characteristics for predicting L2 readability. The integration of these characteristics in the development of predictive models for L2;
- The development of predictive models for L1 using characteristics adapted to the prediction of the readability of this language;
- Using the characteristics of readability measurement to simplify texts. This involves making a text more comprehensible to a reader.

Structure of the these

In order to present the tools and corpora used in the development of our models, to explain the different stages of the processes associated with this development and to present the results of the predictions of our models, we have divided the manuscript into eight chapters:

- **Chapter 1**: This chapter provides an overview of the Arabic language and its morphology. We also give an overview of Automatic Arabic Language Processing (**ALP**). We then detail the notion of legibility and highlight the contributions of ALP in this field.
- **Chapter 2**: In this chapter, we have reviewed a body of work on readability prediction in general. We have devoted most of the chapter to reporting on the state of the art of readability measurement for Arabic texts. We begin by presenting the various traditional approaches based on mathematical formulae. We then presented existing studies based on Machine Learning (ML) techniques. We have also reserved part of this review for work aimed at measuring the readability of medical texts.
- **Chapter 3**: In this chapter we have presented the process and results of developing a frequency dictionary for the Arabic language. From two corpora, one classical and the other modern, we produced four dictionaries using two different morphological analysers.
- **Chapter 4**: In this chapter, we have presented the different corpora that we have developed. We began this chapter with the process and results of developing a corpus for L1. The last part of this chapter was reserved for a presentation of three corpora dedicated to L2.
- **Chapter 5**: In this chapter we have presented the various stages in the development of

models for predicting L2 readability. We have thus detailed the set of features we have adopted to improve prediction quality. Tests carried out on three corpora have shown that these improvements have considerably improved the performance of the readability measure.

- **Chapter 6**: In this chapter, we present the results of using the L1 corpus to develop readability prediction models for Arabic as an L1. We have also presented the set of features we have exploited for this approach, as well as the difference with respect to L2.
- **Chapter 7**: we have devoted this chapter to discussing the contributions of the readability measure in the field of text simplification for L1 and L2.

The final chapter of this manuscript is devoted to a general conclusion concerning all the work carried out, in addition to some future prospects for improving the performance of the models developed.

Chapter 1

TALA and readability measurement

1.1 Introduction

Arabic is one of the world's major languages. It is used by more than 400 million people[3] (according to 2020 statistics), and is the official language of around twenty countries. Moreover, as Arabic is the language of the Muslim holy book, the Koran, it is a language of great religious importance to hundreds of millions of Muslims around the world, whether Arab or not. The areas where Arabic is spoken cover a very large number of countries. This growth in the Arabic population has also led to a remarkable increase in the amount of Arabic content available online. The Arabic language currently occupies the 4®me position among WEB content languages [Boudad et al., 2018]. Not forgetting to mention that Arabic is part of the Semitic language family, and has been the largest member of this group for a long time.

Today, researchers in the field of Natural Language Processing (NLP) are very interested in the Arabic language. In this chapter, we will introduce the different aspects of the Arabic language, as well as the notions of reading, learning and legibility in Arabic as a first language and also as a foreign language. We will then discuss the contribution of Automatic Arabic Language Processing (AALP) to the measurement of legibility.

1.2 The Arabic language

In 1974, Arabic was certified as one of the six official languages of the United Nations, alongside Chinese, Russian, English, French and Spanish. There are two types of Arabic language in general use:

- . Classical Arabic (**CA**: Classic Arabic) is essentially the form of the language found in the Koran; it is also used in classical Arabic literature. This language family is uniform throughout the Arab world;
- . Modern Standard Arabic (**MSA**) is the official language throughout the Arab world. MSA is the form of Arabic currently used in official documents, in educational establishments and for communication between Arabs of different nationalities. However, spoken forms of Arabic vary considerably and each Arab country has its own dialect. MSA is descended from the classical language.

Morphology in linguistics is concerned with the structure of words: how they are formed, and the identity and character of the elements that make them up. Sometimes, words are made up of stems, and more often (especially in Arabic), words are made up of several morphemes. A morpheme can be defined as a minimal unit of form with an independent meaning. Morphemes can be free, meaning that they can stand alone as words, or they can be linked, meaning that they exist only as components of words. In Arabic, most words are morphologically complex, meaning that they are made up of more than one morpheme. The Arabic language is represented by different types of morphemes and by a range of morphological information. These can be summarised in :

- **The word:** this covers the different conjugations of verbs and the declensions of nouns;
- **The stem:** this represents the word without a clitic. It is the result of combining a root with inflectional affixes to indicate grammatical features such as number, person, tense, etc. The use of a stem in a particular sentence is grammatically correct. The use of a stem in a particular sentence is grammatically correct;

---

3 https://www.internetworldstats.com/stats7.htm (last visited 07/11/2020)

- **The lemma:** this represents the entry in the dictionary. It is a specific form that represents the word. The lemma corresponds to the semantic and syntactic composition shared by a set of words. In Arabic, the lemma of verbs is defined as their conjugated form in the 3®me person singular. The nominal lemma is represented by the singular and masculine (if possible);
- **The root:** a set of three, four or exceptionally five unattached letters which together signify a certain abstract meaning;
- **The PoS (Part of Speech):** this is a label providing information on the grammatical category of each lexical unit in a given sentence, in the context in which it appears.

To better explain these morphological representations, we give in table 1.1 some examples of words accompanied by their morphological information.

Word	PoS	Stem	Lemma	Racine
Длу)ДхЛ1у	Name	ДиуДл	ДиуДл	^ у ˉ
^■у|Д^	Name	(J-у/Дл	ДиуДл	^ у ˉ
4jj^j|jjj3	Verb	jjuj'"~j	оу)'-^	^ у ˉ
^-'у)Длу	Name	ДиуДл	ДиуДл	^ у ˉ
^.UJlJ^JI	Name	^^-у/Дл	ДиуДл	^ у ˉ
Ц)1л	Verb	Цу/д3	оу)Д	^ у ˉ

Table 1.1: Examples of words with morphological information

This morphological information is very important in various areas of TALA, including the field of automatic legibility measurement.

1.3 Automatic processing of Arabic

TALN is a sub-field of linguistics, computer science, information engineering and artificial intelligence. It is concerned with the interaction between computers and human languages, and in particular with how computers can be programmed to process and analyse large quantities of data in natural language. It is a set of computational techniques based on theory for the analysis and automatic representation of human language. TALN research has evolved considerably. In the early days of NLP, it could take several minutes to analyse a sentence. Today, millions of web pages can be processed in less than a second. TALN enables computers to perform a wide range of tasks related to natural language at all levels, from syntactic analysis to automatic translation systems.

In recent years, the field of TALA has made considerable progress in a number of different areas and fields of application, which can be broadly summarised as follows:

- **Developing resources:** dictionaries, lexicons, corpora, etc;
- **The basic tools:** morphological analysis, disambiguation, segmentation, morpho-syntactic eti- quing, syntactic analysis, etc ;
- **Applications:** automatic translation, speech recognition and synthesis, character recognition, question/answer systems, teaching, sentiment analysis, etc.

1.4 Legibility

Learning a language can be beneficial to the development of a society. The success of education depends, among other factors, on the quality of the content offered to learners, which must be adapted to their level. It should not be too easy because they might get bored, nor too difficult because they might become completely disengaged. Education professionals in different languages have long used readability measures to help them choose books and other reading materials for their pupils.

It is easy for writers to write texts that respect linguistic rules. However, they may adopt a style of writing that is too lofty and may also underestimate the importance of layout. These aspects, among others, can affect how easy a document is to read for a given reader. A text will be read without undue effort, on first reading, if the reader can decode all the ty- pographic characters and linguistic elements in it. Consequently, the ability to fully process a text depends on two main aspects:

1. Formatting, which concerns the visual presentation of a document (**legibility**);
2. **Readability**, which encompasses all linguistic elements (Lisibilite Linguistique: LL).

1.4.1 Visual legibility

Tracy [Tracy, 1986] defined VL as the ability to read and recognise letters in a clear format. He stated that it describes the comfort of visual processing that occurs during reading. Furthermore, Lieberman [Lieberman, 1967] mentioned in his book that VL is essentially the ease of distinguishing one letter from another. Thus, the LV of characters depends on their design characteristics. For example, a higher 'x' in Latin is considered more legible. Lieberman added that LV is the ease with which the eyes can move and absorb meaning across lines.

High VL is very important for reading because it affects reading speed and the effort needed to identify letters in the correct fagon. However, many factors can play an important role in LV, such as lighting, background and reader fatigue. Low VL can adversely affect the reading process. In [El Kah and Lakhouaja, 2018], the authors mentioned that a set of writing considerations influences the reading process in Arabic learners. Among these considerations they cited:

1. Internal connectivity between letters in the word: detection of word boundaries is affected by blanks or spaces in the word. This specific feature affects the speed of visual processing when decoding and reading words;
2. The different shapes of Arabic letters according to their position in words: each letter can have two to four shapes (beginning, middle, end or isolated);
3. Using points to differentiate graphs ;
4. Diacritical marks: additional diacritical marks appear above or below the letters to express the vowels that help the reader to understand.

Compliance with a set of specific requirements for presenting a text to a learner is increasingly recognised as essential for an effective learning system [Al-Wabil et al., 2010]. The main guidelines for good visual legibility in Arabic can be summarised in :

1. **The interface and colours**: one of the skills that readers need to improve is the ability to maintain concentration [Di tore et al., 2014]. Research has concluded that bright colours and complicated patterns can be distracting, confusing and can generate cognitive overload. Thus, it is recommended to use simple, clear and bold interfaces with light colours to minimise disruption when engaging with readers [Ohene-Djan and Gorle, 2003];
2. **Text form**: many studies have identified and formulated guidelines for formatting text in a way that is more accessible to readers. Recent studies [Chen et al., 2016] [Miniukovich et al., 2017] have concluded that the following guidelines are appropriate for presenting text to learners:
   - Beige background ;
   - Font size 16/18 points ;
   - Black font colour ;
   - 1.5 line spacing and text justification ;
   - Use of bullets and numbering.
3. **Font**: the choice of font is important. For Arabic, Abubaker [Abubaker and Lu, 2012] insisted that the "Traditional Arabic" font should not be used when designing texts for children. For fluent reading, [El Kah, 2019] recommends using the "Simplified Arabic" font with a size of 16 points. For large-print texts, Alotaibi [Alotaibi, 2007] recommends "Times New Roman".

1.4.2 Linguistic readability

LL represents the ease with which a reader can understand a text written on a linguistic level (we will go into more detail about this notion in the next section). Confusion between the two concepts of VL and LL always arises because of a certain overlap and relationship between them. Indeed, when a text is not visually legible, it is not linguistically legible either. However, when it is not very readable linguistically, it is still possible to be very readable visually.

In the remainder of this manuscript, we will concentrate on the LL, which will hereafter be referred to as legibility.

1.4.3 Legibility in L2

With the enormous proliferation of documents available, particularly on the WEB, there is a great opportunity for L1 or L2 teachers to offer texts adapted to the expectations and abilities of their students. In fact, several studies on L1 and L2 readability have been published in different languages. These studies combine NLP and ML techniques to take into account all the lexical, syntactic and semantic dimensions of a text.

One question that arises at this stage is "Why teach Arabic as an L2? Husseinali [Husseinali, 2008] conducted a study to identify why people learn Arabic as a foreign language. His results indicate that L2 learners have a variety of orientations that motivate them to study Arabic: global travel and culture orientations, political orientations, instrumental orientations and cultural identity orientations. There is also an economic orientation; a field that needs people who speak and understand Arabic to conduct economic exchanges with Arabic speakers. The number of people learning L2 is steadily increasing: according to Welles [Welles, 2004], the number of learners enrolled in Arabic courses in higher education institutions in the United States rose from 5,505 in 1998 to 10,584 in 2002. In a more recent study [Looney and Lusin, 2018], the authors mentioned that the number of enrolments for learning Arabic as an L2 is in the range of 20,000 to 30,000. So measuring readability in L2 is a very interesting field of research and also one of the fields of participation of TALA.

1.5 TALA's contribution to legibility

Today, TALA has become the focus of interest for many researchers and developers. In addition, the number of TALA tools and applications has increased considerably in recent years. The integration of these tools will lead to positive results in interactive programmes for learning Arabic.

TALA's contribution to the field of readability measurement began with the use of mathematical formulae known as traditional methods. These readability scores are a way of measuring whether written information is likely to be understood by the intended reader. It is an index that can indicate approximately the level of education a person will need to be able to read a text easily.

The second contribution of TALA to measuring the readability of a text is the use of ML methods. Several studies have been published using this approach. This is generally a supervised machine learning process which involves applying a classification algorithm to text characteristics in order to generate models from a set of pre-classified training texts. The models are then used to classify new texts. The performance of this method depends on the training corpus, the features extracted and the TALA tools used to extract them.

The field of readability measurement, as we mentioned earlier, is based mainly on data annotated by difficulty levels, TALA tools, classification algorithms and other resources such as frequency dictionaries. The use of frequency dictionaries in readability measurement systems is based on the assumption that the more frequent a word is, the more comprehensible it is to readers of a language. These dictionaries support the extraction of a whole category of non-negligible characteristics in readability measurement, which we will discuss in detail in the next chapters.

These dictionaries are lists of the most frequent words in the language in question. The dictionaries currently available focus on lemmas and generally contain a list of the 5,000 most frequent lemmas with their morphological and statistical information. For Arabic, a distinction must be made between CA and MSA lemmas [Reqqass et al., 2019].

1.6 Conclusion

In this chapter, we have presented a general overview of a number of concepts. We have begun by highlighting the different characteristics of the Arabic language and the specificity of its morphology. This morphology is decoded by different types of morphemes, which we have defined in detail. We have focused on an interesting branch of NLD, namely TALA, which has enabled us to discuss the contribution of this field to the readability of Arabic texts. In this chapter, we have identified the difference between two families of text legibility: LV and LL. In the remainder of this thesis, we will focus on linguistic legibility, which will be referred to as readability. In the next chapter, we will review the state of the art of readability.

Chapter 2

Review of literature

2.1 Introduction

The concept of classifying pupils by level originated in America in 1847. Science teachers wanted to teach scientific subjects in simple language, rather than teaching complicated scientific vocabulary. As a result, they felt that measuring readability was essential to determine what seemed readable to their students. Predicting readability is also a privileged way of coming into contact with other cultures and other times, thus enabling the cultural and social development of countries. The development of the Web and the explosion in the availability of information have made it particularly easy to access a large number of written documents, thereby encouraging contact between languages and exposing the public to this linguistic diversity. It is not surprising, therefore, that the choice of materials to be presented at the time of language teaching is a particularly important concern for today's researchers.

The first attempts to assess readability were tests using mathematical formulae. Their main purpose was to measure the level of education a person needed to read and understand a text. They are considered to be simple ways of judging the difficulty of texts.

ML methods are currently widely used to assess the readability of texts. These methods make use of several NLP features.

In this chapter, we will review a body of research that focuses on measuring the readability of texts:

- For L1 learners;
- Intended for L2 learners;
- Dedicated to non-academic purposes.

2.2 Classic formulas and techniques

The classic formulas depend on a set of lexical and syn- taxic characteristics that are easy to calculate. These characteristics include the average word length, the number of syllables in the word and the average length of sentences in words. These formulas have been in use since 1920. Over the years, they have undergone a great deal of development. The underlying message of all these formulas is the same: using short sentences will reduce the level of difficulty and make texts easier to read.

The design process for these traditional formulas can be summed up in four general stages:

1. **Corpus design:** assemble a corpus manually annotated by difficulty level (N1, N2, N3, etc.);
2. **Characteristic definition**: define a list of linguistic characteristics of the difficulty, such as the average length of words or sentences. For each text in the corpus (Text i) we calculate the values of all the characteristics c_{ij} collected (where, c_{ij} denotes characteristic j for text i);
3. **Generation of the formula**: train a statistical model based on the predefined characteristics and the corpus collected. These statistical models are generally linear regressions;
4. **Model validation**: apply the formula obtained to new texts to predict their difficulty levels.

Figure 2.1 shows the flow of these steps to design a mathematical formula for predicting readability.

The beginnings of readability formulas came with the publication of The Teacher's Word Book [Thorndike, 1921]. In this book, Thorndike presented an alphabetical list of the 10,000 most common words in English. In 1944, he published an extension of the Teacher's Word Book containing a list of the 30,000 most frequently used words. He divided this book into two parts. The first part contains words that occur at least once in every million words. The second part contains words that occur at least once in every four million words. The book contains a detailed set of instructions for use by primary school teachers.

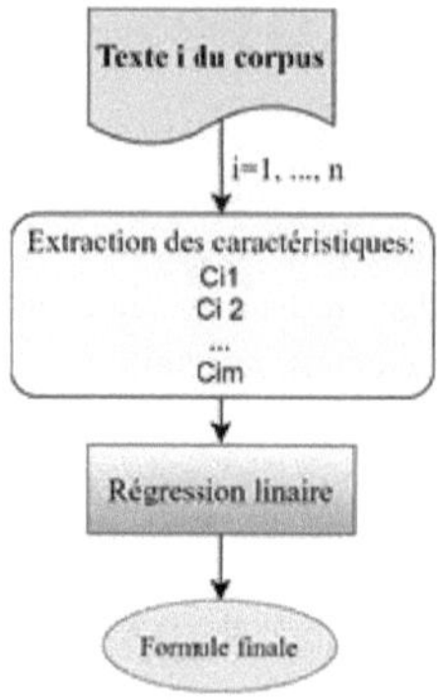

FIG. 2.1 : Steps in designing a readability formula

and secondaries to encourage them to enrich pupils' vocabulary.

In 1948, Rudolf Flesch, the pioneer of readability formulae, published the "Flesch Reading Ease" formula [Flesch, 1948]. This formula, considered to be the oldest, represents a simple approach to assessing a reader's level. The formula is as follows:

$$\textit{Flesch Reading}\ \text{Ease} = 206,835 - (1,015 * ASL) - (84,6 * ASW) \qquad (2.1)$$

or ***ASL*** (Average Sentence Lenght) is the average length of sentences, i.e. the number of words divided by the number of sentences. ***ASW*** (Average number of Syllables per Word) is the average number of syllables per word, i.e. the number of syllables divided by the number of words. The result of the *Flesch Reading Ease* is a number ranging from 0 to 100. The higher the number, the easier the text is to read.

Following Thorndike's book, George Kingsley Zipf published a book in 1949, entitled "Human behavior and the principle of least effort" [Zipf, 1949], in which he established a mathematical relationship between difficult and easy words, which he called "Zipf's law". This law is an empirical observation about the frequency of words in a text. Zipf's law defines the frequency of the word of rank "n" by the formula :

$$f(n) = \frac{C}{n} \qquad (2.2)$$

or ***C*** a constant.

In 1968, a technique emerged alongside readability formulae known as the 'cloze' test [Bormuth, 1968]. Bormuth felt that the readability formulae were too imprecise to be useful to educators. He therefore described in his article how teachers can use the cloze test to determine whether educational material is comprehensible to pupils. The procedure for using the cloze test involves the following steps:

- The passages are selected on the basis of the material, the difficulty of which is to be assessed;
- Every fifth word in the passages is deleted and replaced by underlined blanks of the same length;
- Tests are given to students who have not read the passages being tested;
- Students are invited to write in each blank, without time limit, the word they think is correct;
- Answers are marked correctly when they match the deleted words (ignoring minor spelling

mistakes).
A student's score can be interpreted as a measure of their understanding of the material on which the tests were based.
In 1976, the US Navy changed the "Flesch Reading Ease" formula to "Flesch Grade-Scale" or "Flesch-Kincaid" [Kincaid et al., 1975]. This formula has been used for educational purposes [Marr, 1982]. The formula also uses the number of syllables per word and the average number of words per sentence. According to Flesch, writers can make their texts easier to read by using shorter words and sentences. The *Flesch-Kincaid* formula is defined as follows:

$$Flesch\ Kincaid = (0,39 * ASL) + (11,8 * ASW) - 15,59 \qquad (2.3)$$

Analysing the results of this new formula is very simple. For example, a score of 5.0 indicates that a 5®me year old would be able to read the text, while a score of 9.3 means that the text is comprehensible to a 9®me year old.
Later, in 1983, the Swedish researcher Carl-Hugo Bjornsson developed the LIX formula [Anderson, 1983] to calculate reading difficulty, particularly for L2 texts. The LIX readability formula is defined as follows:

$$LIX = ASL + (LW * 100)/W \qquad (2.4)$$

where ***LW*** (Long Word) is the number of long words (more than 6 letters) and ***W*** (Words) is the total number of words. Unlike the Flesch measure, the higher the score, the more difficult the text is to read.
Other major contributors to readability formulae include Edgar Dale and Jeanne Chall, the creators of the original Dale-Chall readability formula as set out in [Dale and Chall, 1948]. The Dale-Chall formula uses a 'difficult' word count, hence its uniqueness at the time. It calculates the level of a text as a function of the length of the sentence and the number of difficult words. For Dale and Chall, a difficult word represents a word that is not on a specially designed list of common words familiar to most pupils in Year 4®me . The original Dale-Chall formula was based on a list of 763 non-difficult or familiar words and is defined as follows:

$$Dale - Chall = 0,1575 * (100 * AHW) + (0,0496 * ASL) \qquad (2.5)$$

or ***AHW*** (Average number of Hard Words) is the average number of hard words, i.e. the number of hard words divided by the total number of words. In 1995, Dale and Chall revised their formula and extended the list of familiar words to 3,000 words [Chall and Dale, 1995]. The new formula is as follows:

$$Dale - Chall = 64 - (0,95 * 100 * AHW) - (0,69 * ASL) \qquad (2.6)$$

At the end of the 1940s and over the following two decades, other simple readability formulae were developed, such as the Gunning Fog index [Gunning, 1969]. This formula uses complex word counts (words consisting of three or more syllables) as follows:

$$gunning\text{-}foG = 0,4 * (ASL + (100 * ACW)) \qquad (2.7)$$

or ***ACW*** (Average number of Complex Words) is the average number of complex words, i.e. the number of complex words divided by the total number of words.
The SMOG formula [McLaughlin, 1969] has also been statistically estimated from texts and is based on textual descriptors that are easy to calculate as follows:

$$SMOG = 1,0430 * \sqrt{Polysyllabes * (30/Phrases)} + 3,1291 \qquad (2.8)$$

or a polysyllable is a word of 3 syllables or more.
Like the Flesch-Kincaid, FOG and SMOG indices, the Automated Readability Index (ARI) [Senter and Smith, 1967] provides an approximate representation of the American educational

level required to understand a text. The formula is as follows:

$$\text{ARI} = (4,71 * AWL) + (0,5 * ASL) - 21,43 \qquad (2.9)$$

or ***AWL*** (Average Word Length) is the average length of words, i.e. the number of characters divided by the number of words.

All the previous formulas have been used to assign difficulty scores to texts and/or to associate texts with specific levels in school systems. There are currently hundreds of readability formulas for different languages, with varying degrees of accuracy and success rates.

While the English literature is rich and spans almost 100 years, work aimed at explicitly assessing the readability of Arabic is relatively recent. In 1977, [Dawood, 1977] developed the first formula using three text characteristics (AWL, ASL and WF (word frequency)). The formula is as follows:

$$\text{Dawood} = -(0,0533 * AWL) - (0,2066 * ASL) + (5,5543 * WF) - 1,0801 \qquad (2.10)$$

Before the advent of more suitable formulae and techniques, there were attempts to adapt the cloze test for the Arabic language. In 1982, [Hofman and Habib-Allah, 1982] conducted a study to determine whether they should use words or semantic units when applying the cloze technique to the Arabic language. The main aim of their study was to decide whether the elision of whole words, as in English, should be preferred to the elision of semantic units which are whole words in English, but which are not words in Arabic. 1

composed in Arabic. For example, the Arabic word "ببيتهم" / bibaytihim[4] , which means "in their house", should be deleted in its entirety, or only the stem "بيت" / / bayt" should be deleted and the clitics "ب" and "هم". should be retained. In fact, the question was whether Arabic is primarily decoded by perceptual or semantic units.

The tests in the study were carried out on a sample of 584 fifth-, sixth- and seventh-grade pupils from four primary schools. The passages used were taken from a textbook from the Lebanese school system. Each selected passage averaged about 110 words and had been placed by the publisher of the book in the fifth, sixth and seventh grades, respectively. Six tests were carried out as part of this study,

combining each elision method (whole word and semantic unit) with the elision of each 5®me , 6®me or 7®me unit.

Trends in age and frequency of omission tended to favour the whole-word elision method, while the presumed difficulty of the passages was consistent with the semantic unit method. Both methods were found to be valid on the basis of teacher ratings. In summary, the authors concluded that the whole-word elision method seems well suited to Arabic, and there is no reason to abandon this method for use with English and other languages.

In 1984, Al Heeti [Al-Ajlan et al., 2008] developed the second well-known formula for the Arabic language. It considers only the average word length:

$$\text{Al } Heeti = (AWL * 4,414) - 13,468 \qquad (2.11)$$

Choosing such simple characteristics leads to non-performing formulas. More appropriate formulas have subsequently been published. [Daud et al., 2013] presented a formula developed from the Arabic corpus of the King Abdulaziz City for Science and Technology (KACSTAC) [Almujaiwel, 2016]. The latter contains 869,800 texts and 732,780,509 words. The authors classified the corpus by inverse frequency. The word with the highest frequency is ranked last. The proposed formula is as follows:

4 Buckwaiter transliteration: http://www.qamus.org/transliteration.htm (last visited on 07/11/2020)

$$score = TRF/NWS \qquad (2.12)$$

or ***TRF*** (Total Reversed Frequencies) is the sum of the reversed frequencies of the words in the sentence. ***NWS*** (Number of Words in Sentence) is the number of words in the sentence.

In 2014, [Al-Tamimi et al., 2014] published the Automatic Arabic Readability Index (AARI). The authors present an approach based on 1,196 Arabic texts containing 405,408 words from the Jordanian curriculum in the subjects of Arabic language, Islamic religion, natural sciences and national and social education for grades one to ten. The corpus statistics are presented in Table 2.1.

As the Jordanian curriculum is not available in electronic format, they had to type in all the texts manually. Several steps were taken to pre-process the data collected and prepare it for the next steps of extracting characteristics and analysing the texts. The pre-processing steps were as follows:

Level	Characters	Word	Phrases
1	51 076	12 005	2 066
2	65 092	15 592	2 344
3	31 608	6 752	747
4	194 976	46 021	3 453
5	245 661	62 975	4 066
6	210 729	50 714	2 821
7	246 207	58 318	5 825
8	12 046	29 042	979
9	262 495	60 753	4 225
10	262 844	63 236	2 903
Total	**1 582 734**	**405 408**	**27 085**

Table 2.1: Statistics on texts collected by 1 AARI

- Standardising word spacing ;
- Convert letters "(أ />/), (إ /</) et (آ /|/) to (ا /A/)" , et "(ة /p/) at (ه /h/)".

Next, they used three characteristics that have been used and suggested in several readability formulas: NoC (number of characters), ASL and AWL. The first basic formula proposed is as follows:

$$\text{AARI Base} = (3,28 * NoC) + (1,43 * AWL) + (1,24 * ASL) \qquad (2.13)$$

After developing the basic formula, they mapped it to school levels using regression methods and rewrote the formula as follows:

$$\text{School level} = (AARI\ Base + 472,42)/1046,3 \qquad (2.14)$$

In the same year, [Ghani et al., 2014] conducted the first exploration to identify linguistic features that can be used in the development of a formula for measuring readability of Arabic texts among non-native speakers in Malaysia. A sample of 390 learners from all over Malaysia participated in the test. The linguistic characteristics collected were analysed on 15 texts intended for L2. The results indicated that the level of readability of these texts was very difficult. Sentence category was one of the best performing linguistic features in predicting the level of difficulty of the texts. They concluded that in order to develop readability formulas for Arabic texts for non-native speakers in Malaysia, their characteristics can be used as a basis for measurement.

More recently, [EL-Haj and Rayson, 2016] published the **OSMAN** formula (Open Source Metric for Measuring Arabic Narratives). Unlike previous formulas, which do not take diacritics into account, this one does. In this formula, they have introduced a new factor called "Faseeh". A "Faseeh" letter is one of the following: “(ء /’/), (ئ /}/), (ؤ /&/), (ذ /*/), (ظ /Z/)” and the end letters “وا /wA/” ou “ون /wn/”).

They evaluated their method on a corpus of 73,000 sentences taken from United Nations (UN) documents [Ziemski et al., 2016]. The sentences were written without diacritics and in order to count the number of syllables, they added the diacritics using an open-source tool called Mishkal[5] . The formula is as follows:

$$OSMAN = 200,791 - 1,015 * A/B - 24,181 * (C + D + G + H)/A \qquad (2.15)$$

where "A" is the total number of words, "B" is the total number of sentences, "C" is the number of long words (words with more than 5 letters), "D" is the number of syllables, "G" is the number of complex words (words with more than four syllables) and "H" is the number of "Faseeh" words (complex word with any letter "Faseeh"). For OSMAN, the higher the score, the easier the text is to read and understand.

To sum up this section, we have implemented and evaluated the Flesch, LIX and OSMAN formulae on four different corpora (details of the corpora used are given in Chapter 4). The choice of these three formulas is due to the fact that :

1. Flesch is one of the first formulas used in the field of readability measurement, and thus makes it possible to determine the impact of very simple, language-independent characteristics on the evaluation of text difficulty;
2. Lix is a formula that has been applied to the Arabic language in a large number of studies;
3. Finally, we have used the OSMAN formula, as it is one of the latest formulas developed specifically for the Arabic language.

Table 2.2 shows the results obtained with the Flesch formula. For the four corpora, the formula considers that all the texts are difficult.

Table 2.3 shows the results obtained with the LIX formula. The results obtained

	Easy	**Medium**	**Difficult**
Aljazeera-Learning	0%	0%	100%
MoSAR	0%	0%	100%
GLOSS-Listening	0%	0%	100%
GLOSS-Reading	0%	0,7%	99,3%

Table 2.2: Results of applying Flesch to Arabic corpora

with the four corpora are fairly evenly distributed across the three classes.

	Easy	**Medium**	**Difficult**
Aljazeera-Learning	7,7%	27,4%	64,9%
MoSAR	47,5%	32,9%	19,6%
GLOSS Listening	62,55%	37,45%	0%
GLOSS Reading	52,4%	47,6%	0%

Table 2.3: Results of applying LIX to Arabic corpora

Finally, Table 2.4 presents the results obtained with the OSMAN formula. Contrary to Flesch, this formula considers that the majority of texts in the four corpora are easy.

	Easy	**Medium**	**Difficult**
Aljazeera-Learning	58,54%	25,46%	16%

5 `http://sourceforge.net/projects/mishkal/` (last visited 07/11/2020)

MoSAR	97,35%	0%	2,65%
GLOSS Listening	100%	0%	0%
GLOSS Reading	100%	0%	0%

Table 2.4: Results of applying OSMAN to Arabic corpora

We therefore conclude that this type of formula does not work very well and that we need other methods and techniques that offer greater accuracy and performance.

2.3 Assessing legibility through self-learning

Given the weakness of readability formulae, there has been great interest in using ML techniques. The evaluation of readability can be seen as both a regression and a classification problem. However, studies have shown that classification is more accurate and applicable than regression [Feng et al., 2010].

The readability prediction process, based on ML techniques, comprises three main stages:

1. Assembling a reference corpus: the quality and quantity of the texts in the corpus are important;
2. Transformation of corpus texts into feature vectors: the choice of features to be extracted is an essential step in building the prediction model;
3. Application of a classification algorithm to data.

The main difference between the approaches proposed for the automatic assessment of text readability lies in the quality of the corpus, the features and the classification algorithm. With these new approaches, simple features were used in the first ML models for text readability assessment, such as the average number of characters or syllables in words, the average number of words in sentences, the number of sentences in a text and simple language models. The use of more complex syntactic features has also led to more accurate models.

Figure 2.2 shows the flow of the development of these models. The input to the process is the set of texts in the corpus annotated with difficulty levels and morphological information using morphological analysers. The morphological information in the texts, together with other resources such as frequency dictionaries, language models and/or lexicons, is used to extract feature vectors from the texts. These vectors are the input for the learning phase, which consists of training an algorithm on the vectors to generate a model that will be used to predict new observations (texts that are not part of the learning corpus).

The choice of corpus and characteristics depends closely on the type of reader. We have three types of reader:

1. Learners of a language as a first language or L1 ;
2. Learners of a language as a foreign language or L2 ;
3. Readers in general in one language (readers of newspapers, medical brochures, etc.).

In the following subsections, we will first detail the categories of characteristics used in the state of the art, and then present the different algorithms.

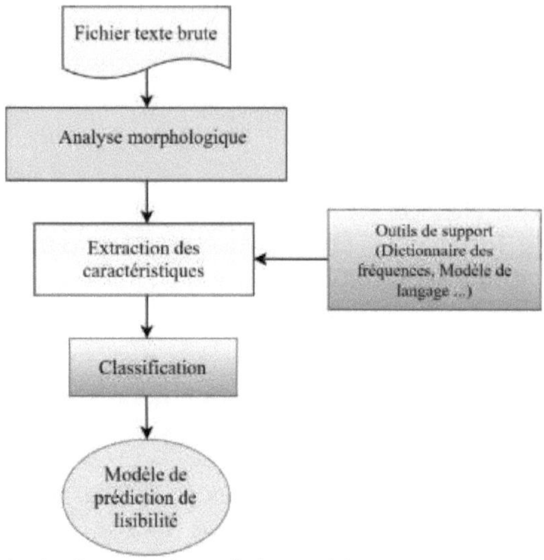

FIG. 2.2: Phases in the development of a prediction model

applied. The learning corpora used in the different studies will be discussed in sections 2.4 and 2.5.

2.3.1 Characteristics used to measure legibility

In this section, we discuss the different linguistic characteristics used in automatic readability measurement techniques. We have grouped them into three families, corresponding to the type of information they are supposed to contribute to the readability model: lexical, syntactic or semantic. Each family has then been subdivided into a number of sub-families as follows:

1. **Lexical characteristics**: numerous studies have shown that the lexical level is the most important source of information for legibility. These factors act essentially at the level of word recognition, i.e. the stage by which a set of features is recognised as a word belonging to an individual's mental lexicon. These factors are as follows:

- *Word length*: the use of average word length dates back to the earliest work in this field. Its use is justified by the hypothesis that the longer a word is, the more difficult it is to decode;
- *Lexical frequency*: word frequency variables are based on the assumption that there is a strong association between the frequency of words in the language and their readability. The most common technique, used by [Dale and Chall, 1948] and others, consists of defining a list of the most frequent words and calculating the percentage of words absent from this list for a given text. A word on this list is considered familiar;
- *Textual plausibility*: this family of variables is also based on the frequency effect, but is approached using n-grams. These aim to estimate the probability that a sequence of words exists in the language;
- *Lexical diversity*: another effect highlighted in the word recognition stage is the word repetition effect. This predicts that word recognition is easier if the word has been encountered previously in the text. By extension, the less varied the vocabulary of a text, the easier the text is expected to be.

2. **Syntactic characteristics**: the syntactic level constitutes a second line of investigation in the measurement of readability, which no longer emerges from the word decoding stage, but already

from the text comprehension stage. Although they are generally considered to be less effective than lexical variables, they improve the performance of the models. We mention three widely used sub-families:

- *Sentence length*: refers to the average length of sentences, which can be measured in characters, words or stems;
- *The complexity of verb forms*: the hypothesis behind this family is that certain verb forms (tenses or modes) are more difficult to decipher than others;
- *Grammatical category ratios*: each text is made up of a series of units belonging to particular grammatical classes. The relative frequency of occurrence of certain grammatical categories is indicative of the difficulty of the texts.

3. **Semantic characteristics**: more recent work has also explored this dimension, without obtaining more conclusive evidence for this family.

2.3.2 Classification algorithms

The classification algorithms used in most works can be summarised in the following list:

- **ZeroR**[3] **(Zero-attribute-Rule)**: the simplest classification method, based on the target and ignoring all characteristics. The ZeroR classifier simply predicts the majority class. Although ZeroR has no predictive power, it is useful for determining a baseline performance that can be used as a reference for other classification methods;
- **OneR**[4] **(One-attribute-Rule)**: a simple classification algorithm that generates a rule for each characteristic in the data, then selects the rule with the smallest total error as the "unique rule";
- **Decision tree algorithms**: the objective of this type of method is to construct a classification function that can be represented by a tree, which is constructed from the root to the leaves. Examples are discriminated on the basis of their classes and the attributes considered to be the best among all the others. Examples used in the state of the art are **J48** [Bhargava et al., 2013] and **Random Forest** [Breiman, 2001];
- **k-nearest neighbors** [Mucherino et al., 2009]: an algorithm that stores all available cases and ranks new cases according to a similarity measure;
- **SMO (Sequential Minimal Optimization)** [Zhao and Yu, 2005]: a fast algorithm widely used for training **SVMs** (Support Vector Machines). The SMO algorithm can be thought of as a decomposition method, whereby a multivariate optimisation problem is decomposed into a series of sub-problems. Each sub-problem optimises an objective function of a small number of variables, typically a single variable. All other variables are treated as constants that remain unchanged in the sub-problem.

2.4 Work dedicated to L2

In 2006, [Heilman et al., 2006] created the REAP tutoring system. A system designed to help learners of English as a second language to improve their vocabulary. The tool defines the level of each document according to the levels of the individual words it contains. It uses **SVM** to obtain a prediction and a simple 'bag of words' approach to determine the level [Collins-Thompson and Callan, 2004]. It provides an estimate of the difficulty of the core vocabulary and can be used as a benchmark to compare other more sophisticated measures and determine the level of contribution.

3. https://www.saedsayad.com/zeror.htm (last visited 07/11/2020)

4. https://www.saedsayad.com/oner.htm (last visited 07/11/2020) of knowledge. Subsequently, [Vajjala and Meurers, 2012] reported on a study in which they tested the impact of lexical and syntactic features deemed significant in the evaluation of linguistic competence in second language acquisition. They achieved accuracy values of around 90% with the 10 best characteristics. Lexical characteristics appear to have a greater contribution than syntactic

characteristics.
In order to answer the question: "Do NLP and ML improve traditional readability formulas?", [Francois and Miltsakaki, 2012] conducted a study in which they compared classical formulas with modern methods that use NLP features and ML techniques. Their experiments were conducted on a corpus for French as a foreign language composed of 408 texts and 127,681 words. They concluded that :

- New readability techniques have produced better results than mathematical formulas;
- The 'non-classic' characteristics were slightly more informative than the classic ones.

In 2019, [Mohammadi and Khasteh, 2019] argued that ML models are highly language dependent and do not perform well for short texts. They introduced the use of Deep Reinforcement Learning models to improve text readability evaluation models. The application of these techniques requires very large corpora, which are not available for all languages.
For Arabic as an L2, most published research has used corpora taken from the Global Language Online Support System (GLOSS[6]). The texts on this platform were developed by the Defense Language Institute Foreign Language Center (DLIFLC[7]), which is considered to be one of the leading foreign language schools. The platform offers thousands of lemons in dozens of languages for independent learners to reinforce their listening and reading skills.
MSA texts in GLOSS are annotated with five levels of difficulty using the Interagency Language Roundtable (ILR) scale [Clark and Clifford, 1988]. The scale is used to measure language skills within the US federal government. The scale assesses people's language skills on levels from 0 to 5. Levels 0+, 1+, 2+, 3+ or 4+ are used when a person's skills far exceed those of a given level, but are insufficient to reach the next level. This means that there are 11 levels in total. These levels can be assigned individually for different skills, e.g. reading, speaking, listening, writing, translating from a written source, and so on. Some of these skills may be denoted by abbreviations, e.g. 'S-1' for spoken language level 1. Table 2.5 lists the ILR levels of difficulty and their interpretations.

Reading level	Interpretation
0	No skills
1	Basic skills
2	Limited competence
3	Professional skills
4	Full professional competence
5	Proficiency in mother tongue or bilingualism

Table 2.5: Interpretation of ILR difficulty levels

In January 2020, the GLOSS platform contained 510 lemons for the MSA. Table 2.6 shows the detailed statistics for this collection.

Level	Reading	Listen to	Total
1	34	44	78
1 +	29	18	47
2	96	67	163
2+	70	63	133
3	49	40	89
Total	**278**	**232**	**510**

6 https://gloss.dliflc.edu/ (last visited 07/11/2020)
7 https://www.dliflc.edu/about/ (last visited 07/11/2020)

Table 2.6: GLOSS-MSA statistics

In 2014, Forsyth described in his thesis [Forsyth, 2014] a system that exploits ML to automatically predict MSA readability. The study is based on a GLOSS corpus comprising 179 texts and 74,776 words randomly divided into three sections: learning, developmental test (devTest) and evaluation (Table 2.7). The learning and development sets represent 80% of the corpus and the evaluation set represents the remaining 20%. The learning and development sets are again subdivided by a further 80/20% split.
To calculate frequency-dependent features, he used a dictionary developed by [Buckwalter and Parkinson, 2014]. Each entry in the dictionary represents a lemma which is accompanied by other information (PoS, frequency, ...). For-

Level	Texts	Learning	DevTest	Evaluation
1	20	13	3	4
1+	14	9	2	3
2	80	51	13	16
2+	40	26	6	8
3	25	16	4	5
Total	**179**	**115**	**28**	**36**

Table 2.7: Statistics on the corpus corpus of [Forsyth, 2014].

syth derived most of these characteristics from this dictionary. To annotate the corpus, he used MADA (Morphological Analysis and Disambiguation of Arabic) [Habash et al., 2009]. He included lexical and morphological features in the model generation process. In total, he developed 162 characteristics. These features represent the vector that will be the input for the learning phase. In this last phase, he used the "Tilburg Memory-Based Learner (TiMBL[8])" system [Daelemans et al. [Daelemans et al., 2004]. On the basis of cross-validation, he reported a maximum F-measure value of 0.52 and 0.78 for five and three classes respectively. The three classes are obtained by grouping together levels 1 and 1+ and levels 2+ and 3.
In the same year, [Cavalli-Sforza et al., 2014] described in their work a study aimed at assessing whether a given text is suitable for a learner of MSA as a foreign language. Table 2.8 summarises the resources they used to design their corpus.

Source	Texts	Word	Lemmas
Al-Kitaab textbook [9]	71	18 784	3 802
UAI Arabic Instructor[10]	23	13 976	3 644
Syrian curriculum	10	10 781	2 659
Online newspapers	10	6 125	1 262

Table 2.8: Statistics on the corpus of [Cavalli-Sforza et al., 2014]

They focused on the vocabulary content of learners' programmes and texts, as well as other word-related characteristics. The model has an accuracy of around 60%.
In 2015, [Saddiki et al., 2015] carried out a study in which they evaluated the usefulness of lexical and morphological features. They also collected a corpus from the GLOSS platform comprising 251 texts and 88,023 words distributed over five readability levels, as shown in Table 2.9.

8 https://languagemachines.github.io/timbl/ (last visited 07/11/2020)
9 Texts taken from the book "Al-Kitaab textbook" part one [Eros, 2005] and part two [Brustad, 2007].
10 Pre-assigned texts by an Arabic instructor

Level	Texts	Word	Lemmas
1	33	6 254	2 192
1+	28	5 128	1 970
2	91	32 438	6 210
2+	63	25 125	5 156
3	36	19 078	4 553
Total	**251**	**88 023**	**20 081**

Table 2.9: Statistics on the corpus of [Saddiki et al., 2015]

They compiled 35 uncomplicated characteristics in order to establish a reference base for future research into readability assessment. Their results suggest that a small set of easily calculable characteristics can be indicative of the reading level of a text. They report a maximum accuracy value of 59.76% and a maximum F-measure of 0.58 using a five-class classification and the Random Forest algorithm. In order to apply classification on data sets that are balanced between classes, they used a three-class distribution like that used by Forsyth. With this new classification of documents into three classes, they obtained a maximum accuracy of 73.31% and a maximum F-measure of 0.73.

Finally, in 2018, [Saddiki et al., 2018] conducted a study in which they used 146 features based on a GLOSS corpus composed of 576 MSA texts. Their best accuracy result was 72.4%, while they obtained a maximum F-measure of 0.61 using SVM and a three-class classification.

2.5 Work dedicated to L1

In 2010, [Feng et al., 2010] conducted a study aimed at predicting the readability of English texts intended for primary school pupils on the basis of a corpus collected from the "Weekly Reader[9] [11] ". They examined a range of features and concluded that PoS-related features, particularly nouns, are individually very useful but highly correlated. They also reported that average sentence length is more useful - and less costly to compute - than individual syntactic features, and that combining these features improved the performance of predictive models. More recently, [Crossley et al., 2017] were interested in predicting comprehension, reading time and text familiarity for adult readers. They examined the use of features that relate to different levels of language: lexical, syntactic and semantic. In their study, they used features more closely related to theoretical and psycholinguistic models of reading than most previous studies. Examples of these variables include the age of word acquisition and the response time of lexical decisions [Meyer and Schvaneveldt, 1971].

Work on the Arabic language began in 2010 with [Al-Khalifa and Al- Ajlan, 2010], who presented a prototype, called "Arability". In order to build their prototype, two tools were integrated:

1. SRILM (SRI Language Modeling) [Stolcke, 2004]: a toolkit developed by the SRI Speech Research and Technology Laboratory in 1995. It is used to build statistical language models that are used in speech recognition, machine translation and other applications. It is used to generate and evaluate a language model based on N-gram statistics;
2. WEKA (Waikato Environment for Knowledge Analysis) [Holmes et al., 1994]: a tool developed by the University of Waikato in New Zealand in 1993. It provides implementations of ML algorithms and contains tools for data pre-processing, classification, regression, clustering, association rules and visualisation.

As for the corpus, they manually collected a set of data from the reading books of the elementary,

11 http://www.weeklyreader.com (last visited 07/11/2020)

intermediate and secondary curricula of Saudi Arabian schools. Their corpus consists of 150 texts and 57,089 words. The texts in the corpus are annotated with three levels of readability: easy, medium and difficult. Table 2.10 presents statistics on the corpus. Five characteristics were used: average sentence length, average word length, average number of syllables per word, word frequency and perplexity score for a dual-gram language model. They obtained an accuracy rate of 77.77%, using an SVM classification algorithm and three levels.

Level	Docs	Word	ASL/Doc	AWL/Doc
Easy	50	4 729	3,95	4,38
Medium	50	24 810	6,37	4,56
Difficult	50	27 550	7,72	4,77

Table 2.10: Statistics on the corpus of [Al-Khalifa and Al-Ajlan, 2010].

In 2014, the authors of the AARI formula (see section 2.2) grouped their ten levels into three classes (easy, medium and difficult), then applied SVM using the value from the AARI formula. They achieved an average accuracy of 83.23%.

In 2018, [Saddiki et al., 2018] conducted a study to predict L1 readability based on the 146 features they used for L2. This study was conducted using a corpus developed by [Al Khalil et al., 2018]. This corpus is composed of 27,688 texts divided into four readability levels. The first three levels were extracted from UAE textbooks, as follows:

1. **Level 1** contains texts from the first to the fourth year;
2. **Level 2** contains texts from grades five to eight;
3. **Level 3** contains texts from grades 9 to 12.

The fourth level contains novels. Their best accuracy result is 94.8% obtained using an SVM classifier on the four classes.

2.6 Comparison between L1 and L2 research in the Arabic language

In this section, we will make a comparison between the corpora and the characteristics of the work carried out on L1 and L2. Table 2.11 summarises the corpora discussed in this chapter. For each corpus, the table presents the authors who have published it, the number of texts it contains, the number of words and whether it is intended for L1 or L2.

Authors	Number of texts	Number of words	Type
Al-Khalifa and Al-Ajlan [2010]	150	57 089	L1
Al-Tamimi et al [2014].	1 196	432 250	L1
Cavalli-Sforza et al [2014]	114	49 666	L2
Forsyth [2014]	179	74 776	L2
Saddiki et al [2015]	251	88 023	L2
EL-Haj and Rayson [2016]	73,000 sentences	1,8 M	L1
Saddiki et al [2018]	27 688	6,9M	L1
Saddiki et al [2018]	576	186 125	L2

Table 2.11: Comparison of Arabic corpora used for readability

Table 2.12 summarises the characteristics discussed in this chapter. It shows, for each work, the authors who published it, the number of features studied and their categories. The categories studied are (see section 2.3.1): lexical frequency (LF), textual plausibility (TP), lexical diversity (LD), word length (WL), sentence length (SL) and grammatical category ratios (GCR).

Authors	No. of variables	LF	TP	LD	WL	SL	GCR

Al-Khalifa and Al-Ajlan [2010]	5	/	/		/	/	
[Al-Tamimi et al., 2014]	7				/	/	
Cavalli-Sforza et al [2014]	7			/	/	/	
Forsyth [2014]	162	/		/	/	/	/
Saddiki et al [2015]	35			/	/	/	/
EL-Haj and Rayson [2016]	6				/	/	
Saddiki et al [2018]	146	/	/	/	/	/	/

Table 2.12: Comparison of legibility characteristics

2.7 Assessing legibility for people with disabilities

People with disabilities experience difficulties with reading comprehension and information processing, which affects their educational attainment, employability and social inclusion. The main objective of this section is to present a body of work that evaluates the legibility of texts for these people, specifically those with :

1. Auditory Processing Disorders (APD) ;
2. Learning disability (LD): people who suffer from dyslexia, dysgraphia and/or dyscalculia.

[Hickson, 2020] is interested in the readability and quality of online information for people with APD. His study was based on 210 web pages specific to English-speaking countries. The readability of these pages was assessed using the FOG, SMOG and Flesch readability formulae. It was found that the online information presented a high level of readability for TTAs. Non-commercial web pages (government and academic sources) showed more obvious readability weaknesses than commercial web pages. He concluded that there is a need to develop new materials that embrace plain language initiatives in order to produce high quality materials that are more comprehensible to this group of people.

For LD, in 2015 [Anoual and Lakhouaja, 2015] reported that an average of around 7% of the Moroccan population suffers from dyslexia, a reading disorder that adversely affects a person's ability to read and understand texts. For this particular population, most research has focused on visual legibility. Few studies have focused on linguistic legibility. In 2009, [Feng et al., 2009] carried out a study of legibility for people with LD based on a corpus of English texts. They collected judgements about the legibility of the texts in the corpus from the target users before designing their predictive legibility model. Their contributions can be summarised as follows:

1. A corpus of texts with readability ratings from adults with LD;
2. A set of characteristics designed to measure legibility;
3. An evaluation of the usefulness of these characteristics in predicting legibility for adults with LD.

Later, [Rello et al., 2013b] presented an experiment, concerning the Spanish language, showing that the use of frequent words and short words improves legibility for people with dyslexia. The experiment involved 46 people, 23 of whom had dyslexia and 23 as a control group.

2.8 Assessing the readability of medi- cal documents

Some studies focus on measuring the difficulty levels of texts intended for non-educational purposes. Medical information, and in particular online health information, is an example of such texts. Several formulas and tools have been used to evaluate the readability of health information in several languages. In 2004, [Gemoets et al., 2004] conducted a study in which they compared two methods for assessing the readability of health documents written in English: the Cloze procedure and readability formulae. The results suggest that automatic readability measurement can provide a reasonable first approximation for predicting the readability of consumer health texts. They also identified several linguistic factors as candidates for improving the performance of automatic readability measurement. Five years later, [Shedlosky-Shoemaker et al., 2009] provided in their study guidelines for assessing the readability and quality of health-related content as well as a demonstration of readability assessment and its limitations.

In [Cronin et al., 2011], the authors assessed the readability of patient information leaflets in Ireland. They used the SMOG formula to assess 45 information leaflets aimed at adults. They found that the majority of the documents were written with an excessively high level of legibility.

To assess the readability of ophthalmic diagnostic web pages written in English, [Edmunds et al., 2013] conducted a study in which they applied four readability formulae: Flesch-Reading Ease, Flesch-Kincaid, SMOG and Gunning Fog. Their results showed that 83% of the WEB pages studied were considered "difficult".

In [Daraz et al., 2018], the authors demonstrate that online health information should reach the reading level of the general public (set at sixth grade level) and that this can help improve the quality of care. The authors conducted a study to assess the readability of online health information in the United States and Canada. The authors evaluated 157 studies and concluded that online health information in the United States and Canada has a level of readability that is not suitable for use by the general public.

For the Arabic language, work on evaluating the readability of health information, particularly medical information brochures, is in its infancy. [Alotaibi et al., 2016] presented a project exploring the possibility of assessing the readability of Arabic medical information brochures using ML techniques. To this end, they developed a corpus collected from :

- **KAAHE** (King Abdullah bin abdulaziz Arabic Health Encyclopedia[12]): an online governmental Arabic encyclopedia on public health;
- **SFDA** (Saudi Food and Drug Authority[13]): an independent government body. They collected drug information leaflets submitted by manufacturers to the SFDA.

The corpus contains 1,112 annotated brochures with three levels of difficulty: easy, medium and difficult.

In 2018, [Al-Aqeel et al., 2018] conducted a study that aims to evaluate the readability of texts about notices, both in terms of vocabulary use and sentence structure. In this study, they use the same corpus as before. The evaluation was carried out by experts and patients at sentence level using three categories (easy, medium or difficult). A total of 4,476 sentences were evaluated, including 2,231 sentences from the SFDA as shown in Table 2.13 and 2,245 sentences from the KAAHE as shown in Table 2.14.

They concluded that for :

- At the SFDA, most of the difficult sentences come from the "What (name of the product) is it and what it is used for" section, which describes the active ingredients, the mode of action, and so on.

	Easy	Medium	Difficult
Experts	1 518 (68%)	534 (24%)	179 (8%)
Patients	1 691 (76%)	369 (17%)	171 (8%)

Table 2.13: Evaluation of SFDA sentences

	Easy	Medium	Difficult

12 http://www.kaahe.org (last visited 07/11/2020)

13 https://www.sfda.gov.sa/ (last visited 07/11/2020)

Experts	1 706 (76%)	384 (17%)	155 (7%)
Patients	1 886 (84%)	247 (11%)	112 (5%)

Table 2.14: Assessment of KAAHE phrases

and indications. In the second order, follows the section "Before taking (name of product)", which describes the precautions and contraindications, followed by the section "Possible side effects".

- On the KAAHE, the majority of difficult sentences come from the "drug interaction" section, followed by the "therapeutic classification and dosage" section, then the "mechanism of action" section.

Their results suggest that the content of the SFDA and the KAAHE is difficult, particularly with regard to side effects and the precautions to be taken in the package leaflets.

2.9 Conclusion

Text readability assessment is a tried and tested problem that is even more relevant in today's information-rich world. In this chapter, we have provided background information on how text readability is automatically assessed, either using classical methods or based on current machine learning algorithms for automatic modelling and prediction of text reading difficulty.

Our review of the field has highlighted the contribution of a variety of published research in the area of readability measurement, both data-based and personalised, as well as test collections and text evaluation measures. We have highlighted the methodological and technical difficulties encountered in developing and evaluating reliable personalised models.

Automatic text readability assessment remains a promising field that tackles the crux of human language comprehension. The need for effective automatic text readability testing will exist as long as there is human language and a desire for people to learn and inform each other, and as long as our computational models of language and language acquisition continue to develop. User-centred, data-driven and knowledge-based text readability assessment is an exciting and promising research direction, deeply connected to our most challenging research problems in human language modelling and interpretation. Advances in the evaluation of text readability will provide the key to a rich range of applications that will help people learn and communicate, whether at primary school or throughout their lives.

Chapter 3

Frequency dictionary for Arabic

3.1 Introduction

Arabic language teaching has spread to almost every region of the world. As this change has occurred rapidly, the field of Arabic language teaching has endeavoured to provide high quality materials and resources. This chapter is a contribution to that effort.

Although textbooks provide vocabulary in every chapter, there is almost never any indication of which words the learner is most likely to encounter in the texts. For independent learners, the situation is even more frustrating. They may pick up a work of fiction or a newspaper and start working through the text by looking up unfamiliar words in a dictionary. But they often have the unpleasant feeling that their time could be maximised if they could start with the most common words in Arabic, using them as a base vocabulary on which to build further reading. Finally, frequency dictionaries can be a valuable tool for language teachers and materials designers. It often happens that learners on a language course have gaps in their vocabulary. In such cases, the teacher often feels frustrated, as there seems to be no systematic way of bringing less-advanced learners up to speed. With a frequency dictionary, learners can work through the list of known words to fill in the gaps in their vocabulary in order to use their time as efficiently as possible. And when designers of learning materials are trying to develop material for their pupils, the frequency dictionary can be used as a guide to assess the difficulty and usefulness of any proposed text or exercise involving vocabulary.

Given that frequency dictionaries are indispensable resources for the development of readability prediction models, and given the unavailability of adapted and freely accessible dictionaries, we present in this chapter our frequency dictionary composed of the 5,000 most frequently used Arabic lemmas. Each entry in this list contains the lemma, its parts of speech (PoS) and summary statistical information on the use of this lemma. The dictionary is based on pairs (lemma, PoS).

3.2 Existing frequency dictionaries

There is a growing consensus that frequency information has a role to play in language learning. Data derived from corpora make it possible to determine the frequency of each word in a language. This information can then be integrated into language learning. Frequency dictionaries have been published in various languages to support teaching, on the one hand, and the development of readability measurement tools, on the other. These dictionaries include: "A frequency dictionary of Portuguese: Core vocabulary for learners" [Silva, 2009], "A frequency dictionary of French: Core vocabulary for learners" [Lonsdale and Le Bras, 2009], and "A Frequency Dictionary of Contemporary American English: Word Sketches, Collocates and Thematic Lists" [Davies and Gardner, 2013]. All these frequency dictionaries present a list of the 5,000 most frequent words in the language concerned.

The questions here are:

- Why take frequencies into account when learning a language?
- Why does a frequency dictionary usually contain 5,000 words/lemns?

In a given language, only about a thousand different words are used in everyday speech. These high-frequency words represent around 95% of the spoken vocabulary. Studies have shown that [Schonell and Meddleton, 1956]:

- The 2,000 words most commonly used orally account for around 85% of written texts;
- The 10,000 most frequently used words represent 99% of spoken language and 98% of written language.

It is important to note that it is impossible to define these figures and statistics with 100% accuracy, but they are nevertheless a global average based on multiple sources [Schonell and Meddleton, 1956].
The size of the frequent vocabulary that learners need to learn is estimated to be around 3,000-5,000 words. According to [Laufer, 1998], secondary school students need a vocabulary of about 3,500-4,000 words. In one of his studies, Laufer indicated that a learner needs a minimum of 3,000 words and a maximum of 5,000 words in order to acquire reading skills more easily. Based on these views, the size of the vocabulary needed to master the English language is estimated at around 5,000 words.
The Arabic language is reputed to have a remarkably rich vocabulary. Various statistical techniques have been developed to verify this, and most Arabic language specialists still agree that Arabic seems to value the retention of a large number of synonyms in the system, and that the overall vocabulary of the language is relatively large. The task of vocabulary acquisition for learners is both more extensive and more difficult, which makes techniques for maximising the time spent learning vocabulary all the more important. A number of experts have suggested that elementary learners should master 750 to 1,000 words, intermediate learners 1,000 to 1,500 words and advanced learners 1,500 to 2,000 words [Tu'aymah, 1986]. Furthermore, [Al-Batal, 2006] estimated that the number of vocabulary words needed to reach a high level of proficiency is between 3,000 and 3,500 words. This amount of vocabulary is sufficient if we consider that learners also need to use dictionaries and morphological knowledge to learn Arabic vocabulary ([Tu'aymah, 1986]; [Al-Batal, 2006]).
[Masrai and Milton, 2017] described in their study an Arabic vocabulary size test used with 339 L1 learners at school and university in Saudi Arabia. The results of the native speaker vocabulary size assessment proved that educated native speakers of Arabic possess a recognition vocabulary of about 25,000 words, a large total compared to the equivalent test results of native speakers of English. Their results also suggest that the speed of acquisition increases with age, which can be tentatively explained by the very regular system of morphological derivation that Arabic uses.
Previously published Arabic language frequency lists have focused exclusively on the formal written language, MSA, but are not publicly available. The frequency dictionaries currently available are seriously outdated and are based on corpora considered to be very small by current standards (represented by millions of words) [Biemann et al., 2007]. In the following, we give a brief summary and description of the existing Arabic frequency dictionaries:

- **The basic word list of the Arabic daily newspaper** [Sprengling, 1943]: this study was carried out to help the teacher and the author of the textbook to determine the vocabulary to be taught to learners wishing to learn MSA. To establish the relative frequency of vocabulary used by the Arabic newspaper, the authors counted over 136,000 words from articles published in Egypt, Palestine, Lebanon and Iraq between 1938 and 1939. The list contains around 6,000 words;
- **"4ш|.£$| 5ДО1 4JL "iU&I alJjaJI" (Essential vocabulary for primary reading)** [JiU-, 1942]: the aim of this study, carried out in 1942, is to help teach the Arabic language in general, reading and dictation in particular, by providing a limited number (about 3,000 words) of vocabulary necessary for a learner to understand more than 90% of the reading books in the first three years of primary school. The work is based on a corpus of 180,000 words taken from 18 primary school books used in six Arab countries;
- **A Word Count of Modern Arabic Prose** [Landau, 1971]: a book which presents a word count of Arabic prose based on twentieth-century Egyptian books. The author incorporated Brill's frequency count, and added a frequency count obtained from a corpus of 136,000 words. The final

list contains 12,400 words;

- **"AJJJxSI ЯxIII ^i 4*JUJI alJjaJI" (frequently used Arabic vocabularies)** [ад^ jjh AJLc, 1979]: a list comprising the surveys of Brill, Aqil and Landau, to which the author has added the results of a survey he made of 255,000 words from Jordanian newspapers and primary school books. The author has limited the list to the 3,000 most frequent words;
- **On the Frequency of Verbs in Modern Newspaper Arabic** [Bobzin, 1983]: a survey which concentrated exclusively on the frequencies of Arabic verbs. The author identified 21,055 verbs in different newspapers published from Baghdad to Algiers;
- **Le Lexique fondamental de l'arabe standard moderne** [Kouloughli, 1991]: a lexicon based on a corpus of 200,000 words taken from newspapers and magazines from all regions of the Arab world, and includes extracts from plays and short stories by writers in MSA;
- **A frequency dictionary of Arabic: Core vocabulary for learners** [Buckwaiter and Parkinson, 2014]: a frequency dictionary that provides a list of the 5,000 most frequently used lemmas in MSA as well as several of the most widely spoken Arabic dialects. The dictionary was generated on the basis of a corpus of 30 million Arabic words that includes written and spoken documents from all over the Arab world. The dictionary provides the user with detailed information for each of the 5,000 entries, including English equivalents, an example sentence, its English translation, usage statistics, an indication of gender variation and the distribution of usage.

All these frequency dictionaries are either not freely available or include dialect data and are therefore not appropriate for measuring readability in the educational domain where MSA is the language of interest. It should also be noted that most of these dictionaries are compiled from small corpora. Since the 1990s, considerable progress has been made in the field of corpus-based computational linguistics, which has made it possible to study much larger quantities of data.

3.3 Dictionary design process

In the course of this research, we developed four frequency dictionaries based on two different corpora:

- The first is a corpus drawn mainly from classic books and represents the CA;
- The second is drawn from a collection of press sites and online books. This second corpus represents the MSA.

In this section, we describe the tasks involved in collecting and annotating corpora and the tools used to develop our frequency dictionaries.

3.3.1 Acquisition of data from the first corpus

Our first two dictionaries were compiled from an improved corpus [Chen- noufi and Mazroui, 2016] of Tashkeela [Zerrouki and Balla, 2017] which is a collection of voiced Arabic texts, most of which are part of CA. The new corpus, named **Tashkeela+**, contains more than 99 million fully voiced words, obtained from :

- **Classical texts**: extracted from the Shamela library[14] and representing the major part of the corpus which is 98.85%. These texts are collected mainly from classical Islamic books;
- **MSA texts**: extracted from the WEB and representing 1.15% of the corpus.

3.3.2 Acquisition of data from the second corpus

Most of the texts in the first corpus are classical, which prompted us to build a new corpus. The new corpus contains more than 59 million MSA words that we have collected from different sources, which can be summarised as follows:

14 http://shamela.ws/ (last visited 07/11/2020)

- **Books**: extracted from the Hindaoui foundation[15] and representing 98.34% of the corpus. These books are collected mainly from children's stories, novels, plays, science books, etc., in e-pub format and then automatically converted into raw text;
- **Web texts**: taken from the web and representing 1.66% of the corpus. These texts are collected from press websites such as http://www.aljazeera.net, https://www.hespress.com and many others.

We have named this second corpus **HindaouiCorpus**. The aim is to select books and texts whose themes coincide with those covered by existing education systems, as well as covering a variety of subjects. Table 3.1 shows the distribution of the HindaouiCorpus by categories. We have a total of 12 categories made up of 1,739 texts and 59,941,592 words.

3.3.3 Corpus annotation

The annotation of the corpora was carried out in two stages:

1. Pre-treatment ;
2. Analysis.

3.3.3.1 Pre-treatment stage

The pre-processing stage consisted in standardising the content of the corpora by eliminating all :

Category	Number of books	Number of words
Children's stories	136	1 645 388
Science fiction	78	1 237 862
Novels	356	14 194 624
Economy	23	1 709 786
Technology	9	858 318
Policy	32	1 848 432
Literature	304	21 995 664
Arts	32	1 358 780
Sciences	68	5 044 922
Biographies	103	7 798 826
Geography	11	1 251 242
Newspapers	587	997 748
Total	**1 739**	**59 941 592**

Table 3.1: Distribution of HindaouiCorpus by category

- HTML tags ;
- WEB links ;
- The figures;
- Non-Arabic words.

We then calculated the number of words, taking into account repetitions, and found that :

- **Tashkeela+**: contains 99,680,874 words;
- **HindaouiCorpus**: contains 59,796,297 words.

3.3.3.2 Analysis stage

To generate the dictionaries, we need to know the lemma and PoS tag for each word in context. To obtain these two pieces of information, we used two morphological analysers, namely :

1. **MADAMIRA** [Pasha et al., 2014]: a system for morphological analysis and disambiguation of the Arabic language that combines aspects of two systems previously used for processing

15 https://www.hindawi.org/ (last visited 07/11/2020)

Arabic, MADA [Habash et al., 2009] and AMIRA [Diab, 2009]. In MADAMIRA, texts go through a pre-processing stage that cleans the text, normalises it, checks its spelling, and converts it into a Buckwalter representation for further processing;

2. **Alkhalil-Toolkit**: a morphological analysis system composed of several independent tools, among which we have used for this task :

- **The Alkhalil lemmatizer** [Boudchiche and Mazroui, 2019]: a lemmatizer for the Arabic language that assigns each word a unique lemma taking into account its context;
- **Alkhalil's PoS tagger** [Ababou and Mazroui, 2016]: an Arabic part-of-speech (PoS) tagger. It offers a very rich set of basic tags to provide syntactic information for each word in the analysed text. In addition, it contains compound tags that allow the analysis of clitics attached to words.

We analysed each of the two corpora using the two analysers. In total, we obtained four annotated corpora. Each word in the four corpora is annotated with a single lemma label and a single PoS label. In Appendix A we present an extract from each of the two corpora annotated by the two parsers and discuss the differences in tags between the four examples.

3.4 Statistical analysis of annotated corpora

From the results of the automatic annotation of the two corpora, we find that for :

- **MADAMIRA**, the Tashkeela+ corpus is made up of 115,344 different lemmas (without repetition), while the HindaouiCorpus is made up of 167,541 different lemmas;
- **Alkhalil-Toolkit**, the Tashkeela+ corpus contains 142,285 different lemmas and the HindaouiCorpus contains 190,242 different lemmas.

For the two corpora, there is a large difference between the number of lemmas found by the two analysers. This difference can be justified by :

1. The error rate due to one or other of the analysers;
2. The normalisation used by the two parsers: sometimes two different words can give rise to the same lemma. For example, for the two words "jUul/<nsAn" and "jUul/AnsAn" ("human being") :

- MADAMIRA will give the same "jU4/<nsAn" lemma;
- Alkhalil-Toolkit will give the "jEul/<nsAn" lemma for the first word and the "jU^l/AnsAn" lemma for the second word.

Hence the significant difference in the number of unique lemmas between the two analysers.

Concerning the discrepancy in the number of different lemmas between the two corpora, this is due to the fact that HindaouiCorpus contains a large set of modern words transcribed from other languages into Arabic, such as the words: "je^>>jA' (Anthropologists)", "Vu^W^l (Electromechanics)", and "A'j-^A^jAi (Chromatography)". These types of words, for which the lemma is sometimes the word itself, have increased the number of unique lemmas in HindaouiCorpus.

Table 3.2 presents a study of the distribution of the Tashkeela+ corpus, by grammatical category of the words that make it up, based on the Alkhalil Toolkit and MADAMIRA tags. Table 3.3 presents the same statistics for the HindaouiCorpus.

PoS	Alkhalil-Toolkit	MADAMIRA
Names	41 563 518	48 685 734
Verbs	20 309 733	18 004 460
Prepositions	7 908 192	12 746 284
Adjectives	13 645 946	4 842 586
Adverbs	1 745 552	531 636
Pronouns	5 473 495	4 587 872

Other	9 034 438	10 282 302

Table 3.2: Type statistics in Tashkeela+

PoS	Alkhalil-Toolkit	MADAMIRA
Names	22 038 947	27 751 773
Verbs	9 815 394	10 782 151
Prepositions	7 078 900	7 468 121
Adjectives	9 400 370	4 468 450
Adverbs	1 388 774	535 491
Pronouns	3 579 302	3 483 264
Other	6 494 610	5 307 047

Table 3.3: Type statistics in HindaouiCorpus

From the results presented in the two tables, we can see that there is a difference between the totals for each grammatical category for the two parsers. For example, some words are annotated by Alkhalil-Toolkit as adjectives whereas they are annotated by MADAMIRA as nouns.

3.5 Dictionary format

The step that follows the morphological annotation of the two corpora is the selection of the 5,000 most frequent "lemma,PoS" pairs.

The dictionaries obtained by the above process contain the 5,000 most frequent lemmas, together with their morphological information. Table 3.4 shows an extract from the dictionary obtained using MADAMIRA on Tashkeela+, and Table 3.5 shows the dictionary obtained using Alkhalil-Toolkit on the same corpus.

Rank	Lemma	PoS	Frequency
1	^3 y^{fi}	Preposition	3 557 342
2	i/min	Preposition	2 670 797
3	j£/EalaY	Preposition	2 573 567
4	ji/>an~a	Subordinate conjunction	2 483 397
5	Jl3/qAl	Verb	2 142 918
6	V/lA	Negative particle	1 767 345

Table 3.4: Results of the frequency dictionary with MADAMIRA

Rank	Lemma	PoS	Frequency
1	^3 y^{fi}	Preposition	3 417 818
2	ji/EalaY	Preposition	2 561 534
3	ji/>an~a	Particle	2 368 727
4	Jla/qAl	Verb	2 067 943
5	V/lA	Prohibition or negation	2 048 404
6	i/min	Preposition	2 041 624

Table 3.5: Results of the frequency dictionary with Alkhalil-Toolkit

From the two extracts of the dictionaries presented in tables 3.4 and 3.5, we note differences between the ranks. For example the couple (j-/min,Preposition) is in position two in table 3.4 whereas it is in position six in table 3.5. The difference is due, as we have already mentioned, to the difference in the sets of labels and to errors in one or other of the analysers. These errors include :

1. In the sentence "le.l£ U^U j£ ^jj (and in each of them there is an intelligence)", the word "^ij/wafiy (and in)" is labelled as an abbreviation by MADAMIRA, whereas it should be labelled as a conjunction "j wa (and)" and a preposition "^a/fiy (in)";

2. In the sentence "d& jl ^ll X>U.V$ (there is no need to be said)", the word "J&/yuqaAla (to be said)" is a verb. Alkhalil considers it a noun, which is incorrect.

For the second dictionary, compiled from HindaouiCorpus, Table 3.6 shows an extract from the dictionary obtained using MADAMIRA, while the extract obtained using Alkhalil-Toolkit is shown in Table 3.7.

Rank	Lemma	PoS	Frequency
1	^ y/fi	Preposition	2 173 161
2	ox /min	Preposition	1 946 633
3	ji/EalaY	Preposition	1 159 318
4	jl/an~a	Subordinate conjunction	1 108 936
5	jl£/kAn	verb	1 074 264
6	J)/<ilaY	Preposition	912 030

Table 3.6: Results of the second frequency dictionary with MADAMIRA

Rank	Lemma	PoS	Frequency
1	^ y/fi	Preposition	2 136 921
2	ox/min	Preposition	1 581 826
3	jl/an~a	Particle	1 217 090
4	o^/kAn	verb	957 451
5	Jl/<ilaY	Preposition	906 369
6	ji / EalaY	Preposition	905 305

Table 3.7: Results of the second frequency dictionary with Alkhalil-Toolkit

For these two extracts too, we have the pair (Js-/EalaY,Preposition) which is in position three in table 3.6 whereas it is in position six in table 3.7.

Finally, in order to give an overview of the four final frequency dictionaries, Table 3.8 presents a comparison between them.

	Tashk_MAD	TashkAlkh	Hindaoui_MAD	HindaouiAlkh
Tashk_MAD	-	42,34%	57,5%	-
TashkAlkh	42,34%	-	-	37,52%
Hindaoui_MAD	57,5%	-	-	53,8%
Hindaoui_Alkh	-	37,52%	53,8%	-

Table 3.8: Comparison between the four final frequency dictionaries

This gives us :

1. 53.8% of common pairs (lemma, PoS) between the dictionaries produced using the MADAMIRA morphological analyser and two different corpora, one classical (Tashkeela+) and the other modern (HindaouiCorpus);

2. 37.52% of pairs in common between the dictionaries produced on the basis of the Alkhalil-Toolkit morphological analyser and using the two different corpora;

3. 42.34% of common lemmas between the dictionaries based on the Tash- keela+ corpus but using two different morphological analysers which are MA- DAMIRA and Alkhalil-Toolkit. The two analysers adopt two different sets of PoS tags, which has led us to report the intersection here

in terms of lemmas only and not in terms of pairs;

4. 57.5% of common lemmas between the dictionaries based on the Hin- daouiCorpus but using the two morphological analysers MADAMIRA and Alkhalil-Toolkit.

The low values for intersections between the four dictionaries are due to the fact that :

- The two analysers use different PoS tags and each has a different error rate, resulting in different (lemma,PoS) pairs;
- The two analysers adopt a different normalisation phase, resulting in differences in the first or last letter of the resulting lemmas. So a common normalisation phase between the two parsers will improve the percentage of intersections between the dictionaries produced using the two parsers.

3.6 Conclusion

In this chapter, we have presented a resource which is essential for the rest of the work carried out in this thesis: the frequency dictionary. This dictionary is provided in four versions according to a combination between the two morphological analysers used and the two different corpora collected. As a result, the dictionaries present a list of the 5,000 most frequent pairs (lemma, PoS) in the Arabic language. This list will be used in the rest of our work to calculate most of the frequency-based features. The list can be used in other fields related to Arabic language teaching.

Chapter 4

Apergu on the educational materials used

4.1 Introduction

Corpora are built for a wide range of purposes such as modelling language use for linguistic research, pedagogical material for educators or learning data for NLP applications. Efforts to create these resources are essential for advancing research in all areas of NLP applications, i.e. morphological labelling, syntactic analysis, machine translation, document classification, etc.

TALA work for MSA is expanding as new resources and tools are developed. Corpus data for MSA comes mainly from the news genre, while there are far fewer specialised resources, such as corpora for educational applications. As a particular type of educational resource, a reading corpus annotated by difficulty levels can be exploited for a multitude of applications: automatic assessment of readability, simplification of texts, language learning, and so on. The creation of such corpora contributes to the diversity of available resources and enables research in TALA to progress in new directions.

In this chapter, we present four different corpora that we have developed and used in our research. The first corpus, called MoSAR (Modern Standard Arabic Readability), is dedicated to learning Arabic as L1, while the other three corpora (GLOSS-Reading, GLOSS-Listening and Aljazeera-Learning) are dedicated to L2. The texts of the four corpora are annotated by levels of difficulty. The L2 corpora are labelled according to five levels, while the MoSAR corpus is annotated by six levels representing the primary school levels in Morocco.

4.2 MoSAR corpus

The main motivation for the construction of the MoSAR corpus [Nassiri et al., 2019] comes from the lack of a freely available Arabic educational corpus, annotated by difficulty levels and intended for L1 learning. Before describing the construction process of the MoSAR corpus, we provide an overview of existing corpora for L1.

4.2.1 Educational corpora used for L1

In this section, we present some popular educational corpora devoted to the Arabic language, and the scales used to annotate the level of difficulty, while pointing out that the Arabic language suffers from a shortage of freely available corpora of this type.

The corpora used by researchers who have studied the readability of L1 Arabic are not as clearly described or easily accessible as the L2 corpora. A few are mentioned below:

- **"Arability** [Al-Khalifa and Al-Ajlan, 2010]: an L1-oriented readability measurement tool already mentioned in Chapter 2, based on a manually collected corpus of 150 texts representing 57,089 words. The corpus is divided into three levels: easy, medium and difficult;
- **"AARI"** [Al-Tamimi et al., 2014]: Automatic Arabic Readability Index (AARI) is also one of the works that are based on an L1-oriented corpus and which is already detailed in Chapter 2. This index was developed from 1,196 texts extracted from the Jordanian school curriculum;
- In their work, [Al-Sulaiti et al., 2016] describe a corpus of reading materials for children. Although the texts in this corpus are classified by category, they are not classified by difficulty level;
- The corpus described in [Al Khalil et al., 2018] consists of textbooks from the curriculum of the United Arab Emirates and covers the curricula from the first year of primary school to the twelfth year of secondary school;

Not all of these corpora are accessible to the public. We mention another direction of corpus production taken by NLP researchers: the construction of learner corpora for different languages. Learner corpora are composed of texts written by language learners. They contain errors and are not useful for reading practice, but can be used to identify common errors made by learners. Among these corpora, we cite the "ALC" corpus [Al-Busaidi et al., 2016] (Arabic Learner Corpus[1]) and the "QALB" corpus [Habash et al., 2013] (Qatar Arabic Language Bank).

4.2.2 MoSAR data acquisition

The texts used in this work were copied manually from the textbooks used in Morocco for the six levels of primary school. It should be noted that there are different textbooks for each level. In addition, the books used are only available in paper format and sometimes there are different versions of the same book. All these factors made it difficult to collect this corpus.
Figure 4.1 shows an example of a raw text from the corpus.

فِي الصَّبَاحِ

سَلْمَى بِنْتٌ نَشِيطَةٌ عُمْرُهَا سِتُّ سَنَوَاتٍ. فَرِحَتْ بِعَوْدَتِهَا إِلَى الْمَدْرَسَةِ.

تُفِيقُ سَلْمَى مُبَكِّرًا كُلَّ صَبَاحٍ. تَذْهَبُ إِلَى الْمَغْسَلِ وَحْدَهَا. تَغْسِلُ يَدَيْهَا وَوَجْهَهَا وَتُنَظِّفُ أَسْنَانَهَا بِالْفُرْشَةِ وَالسَّنُونِ.

"صَبَاحُ الْخَيْرِ يَا أُمِّي. صَبَاحُ الْخَيْرِ يَا أَبِي."

هَكَذَا تُحَيِّي سَلْمَى أَبَوَيْهَا وَتُقَبِّلُ أَخَاهَا حُسَامًا ثُمَّ تَجْلِسُ إِلَى الْمَائِدَةِ مَعَ أُسْرَتِهَا.

FIG. 4.1: Example of MoSAR plain text

4.2.3 Annotation of the MoSAR corpus

To generate the final annotated corpus, we followed five steps:

1. **Manual editing and assembly:** the texts collected manually are typed and assembled in text files, then manually checked to correct any typing errors;

2. http://www.arabiclearnercorpus.com/ (last visited 08/11/2020)

3. **First annotation phase:** we collected the different text files into six files, with each file representing one school level. We annotated the files manually with different information such as the level, the title of the book, the title of the text, etc. We then generated XML and JSON files from the text files. Figure 4.2 shows an extract from the first XML file (level 1);

```xml
<?xml version-'1.0' encoding-'UTF 8'>

<book id='1' title='كتابي في اللغة العربي' level='1'>

    <text id='1' week='1' type='Expression' title='في الصباح'>

في الصَّبَاحِ

سَلْمَى بِنْتٌ نَشِيطَةٌ عُمْرُهَا سِتُّ سَنَوَاتٍ. فَرِحَتْ بِعَوْدَتِهَا إِلَى الْمَدْرَسَةِ.

تُفِيقُ سَلْمَى مُبَكِّرًا كُلَّ صَبَاحٍ. تَذْهَبُ إِلَى الْمَغْسَلِ وَحْدَهَا. تَغْسِلُ يَدَيْهَا وَوَجْهَهَا وَتُنَظِّفُ أَسْنَانَهَا
بِالْفُرْشَةِ وَالْمَعْجُونِ.

" صَبَاحُ الْخَيْرِ يَا أُمِّي. صَبَاحُ الْخَيْرِ يَا أَبِي".

هَكَذَا تُحَيِّي سَلْمَى أَبَوَيْهَا وَتُقَبِّلُ أَخَاهَا حَسَنًا ثُمَّ تَجْلِسُ إِلَى الْمَائِدَةِ مَعَ أُسْرَتِهَا.

    </text>

    ...

</book>

...
```

FIG. 4.2: Example of a manually annotated text in XML format

4. **Second annotation phase:** as shown in Figure 4.3, each raw text from the first annotation phase is analysed by the AlKhalil-Toolkit tools (stemmer, lemmatizer, PoS-tagger and root). The morphological information obtained is added to the information from the first annotation phase to obtain the final annotated corpus, in XML format, which we have named MoSAR (Modern Standard Arabic Readability);

5. **Manual validation of annotations:** during this stage, we manually checked around 10% of the texts (selected randomly) to detect the presence of incorrect tags. Table 4.1 shows an analysis of the PoS tags of 58 texts representing 7,006 words. Indeed, we found some errors such as the attribution of the "Adjective" tag to nouns with a total of 14.25%;

Type	Analysis results		Accuracy	Error rate
	Number of words	Percentage		
Names	3 115	44,46%	98,29%	1,7%
Verbs	1 342	19,15%	92,10%	7,89%
Preposition	598	8,53%	100%	0%
Adjectives	975	13,91%	85,74%	14,25%
Pronouns	301	4,29%	100%	0%
Adverbs	123	1,75%	100%	0%
Other	552	7,87%	100%	0%
Total	**7 006**	**100%**	**95,27%**	**4,73%**

Table 4.1: Statistics on the 10% of MoSAR validation data

6. **Format conversion:** the final corpus is converted to JSON and text formats.

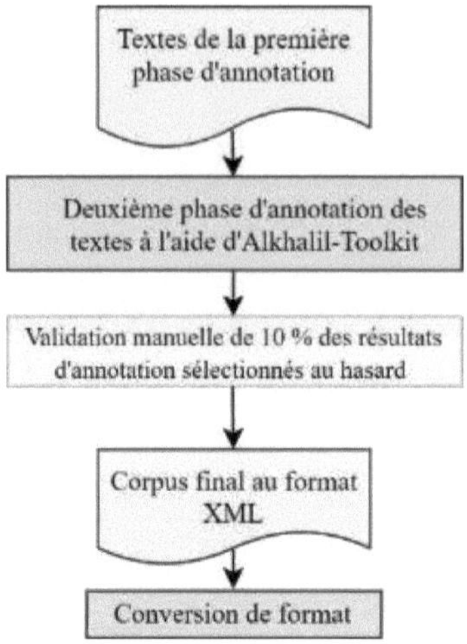

FIG. 4.3: Annotation process for the MoSAR corpus

Figure 4.4 shows an extract of a sentence from the corpus annotated in XML format. This sentence is taken from the example in Figure 4.1.
In Appendix B we present an extract from the corpus in JSON and plain text formats.

```
<segment_info id='4'>
    <sentence> تفيق سلمى مبكرا كل صباح. </sentence>
    <analysis nb='5'>
        <morph_feature_set id='1' word=' تفيق ' stem='تفيق' lemma='[illegible]' root='[illegible]' pos='VcP' />
        <morph_feature_set id='2' word=' سلمى ' stem='سلمى' lemma='سلمى' root='-' pos='Alam' />
        <morph_feature_set id='3' word=' مبكرا ' stem='مبكرا' lemma='مبكر' root='بكر' pos='Sifa' />
        ...
    </analysis>
</segment_info>
...
```

FIG. 4.4: XML format of the annotated corpus

4.2.4 Statistical analysis of the MoSAR corpus

In this section, we highlight the characteristics of the MoSAR corpus using a number of statistical analyses. In total, this corpus consists of 602 texts comprising 7,553 sentences and 77,966 words, taking repetitions into account.

Table 4.2 presents some detailed information on the MoSAR corpus, such as the number of books per level, the number of texts, etc.

Level	Books	Texts	Phrases	Word	Stems	Lemmas	Roots
1	1	51	526	3 090	1 440	1 185	827
2	2	139	1 713	12 988	4 769	3 630	2 240
3	1	60	909	9 897	4 101	3 237	2 037
4	2	136	1 872	24 619	8 176	6 277	3 485

5	1	86	1 193	14 251	5 982	4 798	2 769
6	1	130	1 340	13 121	5 236	4 311	2 570
Total	**8**	**602**	**7 553**	**77 966**	**17 587**	**12 477**	**6 739**

Table 4.2: Detailed information on the MoSAR corpus

The length of the words the learner encounters when deciphering a text influences the legibility and clarity of the text read. Several studies on different languages have shown that the average word length varies from 7 to 12 letters[16] . For Arabic, the average word length in a normal text has been estimated at five letters [Mustafa, 2012]. In Table 4.3, we present a statistical study of word length broken down by levels (from one to six), giving an overview of the distribution of word sizes in each level. The average word size in the MoSAR corpus is 4.5 letters.

Number of letters	N1	N2	N3	N4	N5	N6
1	0	1	3	7	7	4
2	37	69	67	105	83	78
3	194	533	466	855	639	588
4	433	1 458	1 143	2 405	1 697	1 435
5	410	1 576	1 324	2 975	1 911	1 613
6	326	1 252	1 070	2 343	1 555	1 380
7	196	798	670	1 378	992	882
8	63	346	256	535	433	372
9	23	75	79	175	155	110
10	1	7	28	45	37	26
Only 10 more to go	0	1	5	10	9	7
Average length	**4,59**	**4,54**	**4,55**	**4,43**	**4,59**	**4,48**

Table 4.3: Word length statistics (distinct words)

The identification of frequent words makes it possible to indicate the distribution of vocabulary in the corpus and the familiarity of the words it contains. Frequent words are calculated using PoS tags and lemmas instead of words. Obviously, prepositions and articles will be at the top of the list of frequent words. Table 4.4 shows the distribution of the MoSAR corpus in relation to the two frequency dictionaries based on Alkhalil-Toolkit which we presented in the previous chapter. We chose these dictionaries for the correspondence of the tags with the corpus. For this table, a frequent word is a word in the corpus whose (lemma,PoS) pair appears in the frequency dictionary. For the first level, for example, we have 621 pairs (lemma,PoS) which belong to the first dictionary (based on Tashkeela+), while we have 797 pairs which belong to the second dictionary (based on HindaouiCorpus).

Level	**Total couples (C)**	**Dictionary 1**		**Dictionary 2**	
		C common	**Percentage**	**C common**	**Percentage**
1	1 655	621	37,5%	797	48,15%
2	5 943	1 519	25,55%	1 965	33,06%
3	5 011	1 420	28,33%	1 911	38,13%
4	10 548	2 384	22,60%	3 158	29,93%
5	7 352	1 954	26,57%	2 645	35,97%
6	6 403	1 794	28,01%	2 388	37,29%

16 http://www.ravi.io/language-word-lengths (last visited 08/11/2020)

Total	24 890	3 259	4	L80

Table 4.4: Statistics on the distribution of frequent words in MoSAR

It is clear from the results in Table 4.4 that the second dictionary covers more of the vocabulary in the corpus, with a total of 4,180 pairs, whereas the first dictionary covers only 3,259 pairs in the corpus. We can therefore expect the readability results to improve if we use the second dictionary instead of the first.

Finally, Table 4.5 gives an overview of the distribution of the Mo- SAR corpus by grammatical category, based on the Alkhalil-Toolkit tags.

PoS	Number of words	Percentage
Names	32 165	41,25%
Verbs	15 036	19,28%
Preposition	11 145	14,29%
Adjectives	11 244	14,42%
Pronouns	1 727	2,21%
Adverbs	1 588	2,03%
Other	5 061	6,52%

Table 4.5: Type statistics in MoSAR

The results of this statistical study show that the main grammatical category in MoSAR is nouns, followed by verbs.

4.2.5 Advantages and limitations of the MoSAR corpus

Compared with existing freely available educational corpora, our corpus offers the following advantages:

- It is intended for L1 learners, whereas the best-known corpora available are intended for L2 learners;
- We propose a sufficient number of texts for the application of machine learning techniques;
- The corpus is made up of texts corresponding to six primary school levels, which gives an indication of the difficulty of the texts.

An obvious limitation of the corpus is its restriction to Moroccan primary school levels and the absence of texts from other subjects such as Islamic education, technology and mathematics. It would be desirable to add texts from higher levels covering all subjects. Nevertheless, the emphasis on the early grades is justified because strong reading skills are most useful when acquired early in school. Children who finish Year 3 with below-average reading skills are at high risk of suffering academically overall, as the extra effort required to read prevents them from keeping up with the pace of learning required in other courses [McClelland et al., 2006]. Consequently, a resource dedicated to early grades remains a valuable support for teachers, learners and educational researchers.

4.2.6 Other applications of the MoSAR corpus

As well as measuring readability, the MoSAR corpus can be used in other areas:

Making learning attractive: as reading is a crucial skill in edu- cation, it is essential to develop a love of reading in children. In [El Kah et al., 2017], the authors created games for learning Arabic using TALA tools and resources. MoSAR offers a resource that can support such work. It will facilitate the choice of words, sentences presented to learners for each learning level, and the creation of datasets for these games.

Evaluation of the current reading programme: finally, the MoSAR corpus, insofar as it reflects the existing reading programme in Moroccan primary schools, will provide an opportunity to critically evaluate such a programme. We have carried out a study whose aim is to follow a learner's vocabulary learning throughout primary school from year 1er to year 6ème. In Table 4.6, we present a statistical study of the new lemmas the learner encounters in each level (ignoring those already encountered in previous levels). These statistics are based on one book per level.

Level	Lemmas	Cumulative lemmas	New lemmas
1	1 185	1 185	-
2	2 029	2 651	1 466
3	3 237	4 627	1 976
4	3 780	6 654	2 027
5	4 798	8 985	2 331
6	4 311	10 730	1 745
Total	**10 730**	-	-

Table 4.6: Vocabulary statistics in MoSAR

We note that the new lemmas acquired from one level to the next are increasing, with the exception of the last level. Based on these results, a learner finishes primary school in Morocco with a vocabulary of 10,730 lemmas, a large total compared with the results for other languages. For example, the size of the vocabulary needed to master English is estimated at around 5,000 words.

In order to compare the vocabulary acquired by two learners at the same school level but learning from two different books, we compared the lemmas from the two different books from the second and fourth levels of the MoSAR corpus. Table 4.7 presents the results of this comparison and we note that :

- For the second level: the intersection between the two books is 821 lemmas, which represents approximately 32% of common lemmas and a difference of 68%;
- For the fourth level: we have an intersection of 1,495 lemmas, which represents 36% common lemmas and a difference of 64%.

It is clear from these results that two learners at the same level using different books do not learn the same vocabulary.

Level	Lemmas book 1	Lemmas book 2	Intersection (%)	Difference (%)
2	2 029	2 533	32%	68%
4	3 780	4 109	36%	64%

Table 4.7: Comparison of the vocabulary of two different books at the same level

When we designed the MoSAR corpus, we noticed that there were no books for all levels in the same edition. As a result, learners do not finish primary school with the same vocabulary.

4.3 L2 corpus

Learning a second language is an essential part of modern life and a goal of many education systems around the world.

In this section, we will present in detail three corpora annotated by difficulty level and dedicated to learning Arabic as an L2.

4.3.1 General context

We already mentioned in the previous section that the field of readability measurement suffers from a great lack of data annotated by difficulty level, which is a major obstacle to the development of effective tools in this field. For L2, offers are even rarer. To the best of our knowledge, the only platforms offering texts specifically for L2 learners are :

- The GLOSS platform. These texts are already discussed in chapter 2 and are used in several previous studies;
- Texts available online from Aljazeera[17] . The Aljazeera-Learning website for learning Arabic also features educational texts. This resource consists of three categories of texts: "Media language", "General language" and "Our community". The texts in each of these three categories are annotated by five levels of difficulty: Beginner1, Beginner2, Intermediate1, Intermediate2 and Advanced.

4.3.2 Methodology and tools

In this section, we present the process of collecting and annotating three corpora that we will subsequently use in the development of L2 readability prediction models, namely: GLOSS-Reading, GLOSS-Listening and Aljazeera-Learning.

4.3.2.1 Data acquisition

Our first two corpora are collected from the study programme put on line by the DLIFLC, the main language teaching establishment for members of the US armed forces. Their site is open to the public and includes several teaching materials in different languages. The GLOSS corpora contain MSA documents classified by the authors according to the standard levels of the ILR, which was developed to describe the ability to communicate in a language, particularly in the context of learning a second language. As already mentioned, the ILR assesses language skills using a scale from 0 to 5. A '*plus*' level (0+, 1+, 2+, 3+ and 4+) is assigned when the required skills exceed a given level, but do not allow full access to the next level. The texts we collected range from ILR level 1 (basic competence) to ILR level 3 (general professional competence). We have collected two corpora from this resource:

- **GLOSS-Reading**: a corpus of reading lemons. It represents a valuable resource for maintaining and improving learners' language skills. The corpus has a total of 271 documents and 95,496 words;
- **GLOSS-Listening**: a corpus composed of texts obtained from listening material such as television reports, radio broadcasts, etc. The corpus has a total of 227 documents and 56,684 words.

Our latest L2 corpus is collected from texts posted on the Aljazeera-Learning website. A website that provides a space for practising and improving the Arabic language. It will help learners to learn by offering a range of interactive activities. The site is dedicated to adults learning Arabic as a foreign language. It does not contain any learning materials for children. It is intended for those who can at least read and write the Arabic alphabet. To make it easier to present the results, we will use levels 1 (Beginner1), 1+ (Beginner2), 2 (Intermediate1), 2+ (Intermediate2) and 3 (Advanced).

Figure 4.5 shows an example of a plain text intended for L2. This text is taken from the Aljazeera-Learning corpus.

17 https://learning.aljazeera.net (last visited 08/11/2020)

إدمان الإنترنت

قالت الجمعية الألمانية للطب النفسي إن إدمان الإنترنت غالبا ما يقترن بأمراض نفسية أخرى.

فعلى سبيل المثال يستخدم مرضى الاكتئاب الإنترنت بشكل مفرط من أجل مواجهة مشاعر الوحدة التي تنتابهم، ولذلك ينبغي فحص المصابين بإدمان الإنترنت لاكتشاف ما إذا كانوا يعانون من أمراض نفسية أخرى.

وأضافت الجمعية أن أعراض الإدمان تتمثل في التالي:

-فقدان السيطرة على استخدام الإنترنت.

-الشعور بالقلق والتوتر الداخلي من دون الإنترنت.

-إهمال الهوايات والاهتمامات.

FIG. 4.5: Example of a plain text from Aljazeera-Learning

4.3.2.2 Corpus annotation

The three corpora we collected will be used in the rest of this thesis to generate readability prediction models. We annotated these texts with PoS tags and lemmas using MADAMIRA (Figure 4.6) and Alkhalil-Toolkit (Figure 4.7). The input for this step is the collection of corpus texts in plain text format. We use the morphological information obtained from the parsers, to which we add the original difficulty level of the text, to obtain the annotated corpora that we will use in the rest of this thesis.

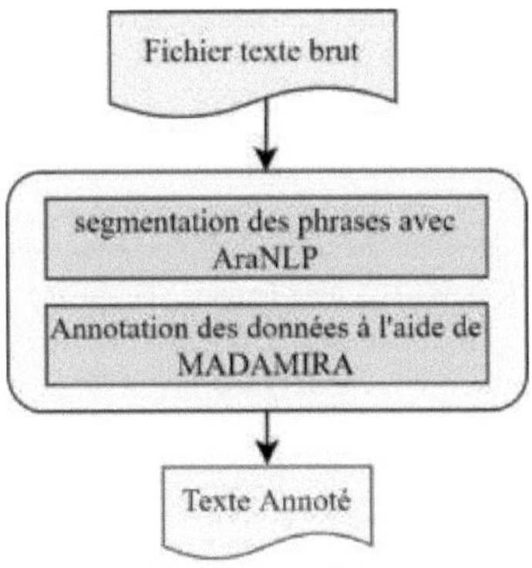

FIG. 4.6: L2 corpus annotation process with MADAMIRA

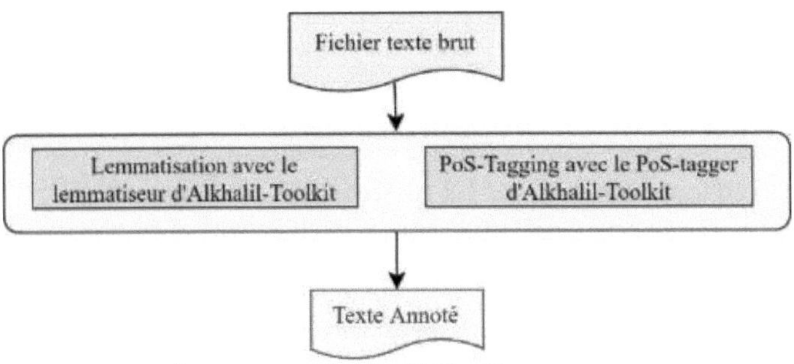

FIG. 4.7: L2 corpus annotation process with Alkhalil-Toolkit

After this annotation phase, we calculated for each corpus the number of sentences, the number of words, the number of lemmas, and the number of new lemmas encountered by the learner in the different levels. Table 4.8 presents the results of these statistics for the GLOSS-Reading corpus. The distribution of texts between the levels of this corpus is not homogeneous.

Level	Texts	Phrases	Word	Lemmas (L)	Cumulative L	New L
1	34	920	6 313	1 958	1 958	-
1 +	29	317	5 149	1 747	2 868	910
2	95	1 406	33 264	5 331	6 278	3 410
2+	68	1 033	27 175	4 560	7 730	1 452
3	45	990	23 595	4 322	8 841	1 111
Total	**271**	**4 666**	**95 496**	**8 841**	-	-

Table 4.8: Statistics for the GLOSS-Reading corpus with MADAMIRA

GLOSS-Reading is composed of 271 texts, 4666 sentences and 95,496 words, whereas the GLOSS-Listening corpus is composed of 227 texts, 5,457 sentences and 56,684 words as shown in Table 4.9. This second corpus also has a non-homogeneous distribution of texts between levels.

Level	Texts	Phrases	Word	Lemmas	Cumulative L	New lemmas
1	43	2 171	9 148	1 747	1 747	-
1 +	18	301	3 280	1 178	2 392	645
2	65	796	12 611	3 071	4 220	1 828
2+	62	1 226	17 834	3 372	5 614	1 394
3	39	963	13 811	2 920	6 542	928
Total	**227**	**5 457**	**56 684**	**6 542**	-	-

Table 4.9: Statistics for the GLOSS-Listening corpus with MADAMIRA

Table 4.10 shows the distribution of the Aljazeera-Learning corpus by level, as well as the number of words, sentences, lemmas and new lemmas, as for the other two corpora. Aljazeera-Learning consists of 321 texts, 2,442 sentences and 49,345 words. With regard to the distribution of this corpus, the situation is even more frustrating given the great imbalance of texts between the five levels. The majority of texts are concentrated in level 1+, with 220 texts, while the remaining 101 texts are spread across the other four levels.

Level	Texts	Phrases	Word	Lemmas	Cumulative L	New lemmas
1	12	176	942	475	475	-
1 +	220	1 101	20 898	4 278	4 409	3 934
2	54	378	7 646	2 358	5 138	729
2+	27	608	15 191	3 443	6 324	1 186
3	8	179	4 668	1 636	6 672	348
Total	**321**	**2 442**	**49 345**	**6 672**	-	-

Table 4.10: Statistics for the Aljazeera-Learning corpus with MADAMIRA

4.3.3 Statistical analysis of L2 annotated corpora

In this section, we will present and detail some statistical analyses of the characteristics of our three collected and annotated corpora.

The first piece of information we will report is the distribution of grammatical categories of words in the three corpora. We report this analysis based on the Alkhalil-Toolkit and MADAMIRA tags. Tables 4.11 and 4.12 present the results of this analysis on the GLOSS-Reading, GLOSS-Listening and Aljazeera-Learning corpora.

PoS	GLOSS-Reading	GLOSS-Listening	Aljazeera-Learning

	Word	Percentage	Word	Percentage	Word	Percentage
Names	51 526	53,95%	31 052	54,78%	27 524	53,95%
Verbs	11 830	12,38%	6857	12,09%	5 936	11,63%
Preposition	11 008	11,52%	6064	10,69%	5 556	10,89%
Adjectives	11 005	11,52%	6 127	10,80%	5 900	11,56%
Adverbs	716	0,74%	628	1,10%	312	0,61%
Pronouns	4 145	4,34%	2 766	4,87%	1 852	3,63%
Other	5 266	5,55%	3 190	5,67%	3 932	7,73%

Table 4.11: Statistics on PoS with MADAMIRA in L2

PoS	GLOSS-Reading		GLOSS-Listening		Aljazeera-Learning	
	Word	Percentage	Word	Percentage	Word	Percentage
Names	42 887	44,90%	25 749	45,42%	22 456	45,50%
Verbs	11 010	11,52%	6 302	11,11%	5 529	11,20%
Preposition	10 166	10,64%	6 319	11,14%	5 749	11,65%
Adjectives	19 860	20,79%	11 795	20,80%	10 636	21,55%
Adverbs	2 534	2,65%	1 503	2,65%	1 276	2,58%
Pronouns	3 696	3,87%	2 152	3,79%	1 674	3,39%
Other	5 343	5,63%	2 864	5,09%	2025	4,13%

Table 4.12: Statistics on PoS with Alkhalil-Toolkit in L2

From the results presented in the two tables, we can see that there is a difference between the totals for each grammatical category for the two parsers. Some words are annotated by Alkhalil-Toolkit as adjectives whereas they are annotated by MADAMIRA as nouns.

Finally, Tables 4.13 and 4.14 present the results of the frequency analysis in the three L2 corpora. These are statistics on the number of frequent words belonging to the two dictionaries (CA and MSA), broken down by level.

Level	GLOSS-Reading		GLOSS-Listening		Aljazeera-Learning	
	Couples	Percentage	Couples	Percentage	Couples	Percentage
1	957	30,72%	994	31,65%	293	48,03%
1+	907	32,55%	643	36,93%	1 852	21,33%
2	2 150	18,36%	1 484	26,17%	1 221	29,87%
2+	2 028	20,13%	1 677	24,69%	1 628	24,28%
3	2 017	21,80%	1 538	28,07%	856	33,17%
Total	**3 050**		**2 643**		**2 625**	

Table 4.13: Statistics on the distribution of frequent words in L2 compared with the classic dictionary

Level	GLOSS-Reading		GLOSS-Listening		Aljazeera-Learning	
	Couples	Percentage	Couples	Percentage	Couples	Percentage
1	1 328	42,63%	1 270	40,44%	370	60,65%
1+	1 282	46,01%	880	50,54%	2 600	29,95%
2	3 094	26,42%	2 111	37,23%	1 735	42,45%
2+	2 877	28,55%	2 295	33,79%	2 311	34,47%
3	2 828	30,57%	2 014	36,75%	1 201	46,55%
Total	**4 115**		**3 541**		**3 571**	

Table 4.14: Statistics on the distribution of frequent words in L2 compared with the modern

dictionary

For all three corpora, the second dictionary covers more vocabulary than the first dictionary. Again, based on these statistics, we expect the readability measurement results based on the second dictionary to be better than those obtained using the first dictionary.

4.4 Conclusion

In this chapter, we have presented a new corpus of Arabic educational texts for L1 learners. One of the advantages of this corpus is that it provides a more abundant collection of texts than the few comparable corpora available. Another advantage is that the texts are annotated with difficulty levels based on the primary levels of the Moroccan school system, and with rich morphological information produced by Alkhalil-Toolkit. This corpus can be used to train, optimise and evaluate approaches in the field of readability measurement for L1 learners, to support the development of language learning games, and to evaluate the quality of the reading material and the reading programme itself.

The current corpus can be further improved by increasing the number of texts and extending the corpus to higher school levels and other disciplines.

Finally, we presented three corpora of Arabic educational texts for L2 learners: GLOSS-Reading, GLOSS-Listening and Aljazeera-Learning. These three corpora represent the standard data most commonly used in the development of readability prediction models for texts intended for foreign learners of the Arabic language. The texts of all these corpora are annotated with five levels of difficulty, and we have also annotated them with rich morphological information.

Chapter 5

Measuring readability in L2

5.1 Introduction

Assessing the readability of texts is an important task in foreign language teaching. If carried out manually, this process can be time-consuming and expensive, which limits its application. For this reason, in recent years there has been growing interest in developing models for automatically predicting the readability of foreign language learning texts.

The combination of TALA and ML techniques in readability prediction requires three main steps: the first step consists in gathering a reference corpus, the second step consists in identifying and extracting from the corpus a set of linguistic characteristics, also called predictors, in order to use them in combination with ML algorithms. The final stage consists of a classification phase. The predictors obtained in the second stage must have a significant correlation, or even a causal relationship, with the difficulty of the texts.

In this chapter, we first considered predicting readability with a large set of features inspired by the Arabic readability prediction literature. Then, we tried to ignore some features that seemed less relevant than expected, in order to obtain prediction results of comparable accuracy with a reduced set of features. These studies were carried out using three different corpora dedicated to the learner of Arabic as an L2: Aljazeera-Learning, GLOSS-Reading and GLOSS-Listening.

5.2 Complete set of features

The characteristics of the text associated with its degree of difficulty present a range of complexity in terms of ease of retrieval. Simple features include language-independent attributes such as text length, sentence length or average word length. Complex or higher-level features represent those that are dependent on the language being processed.

In reviewing the state of the art of readability studies, we have found several interesting categories of features, including frequency based on grammatical categories, lemma/PoS ratio, word and lemma frequency, word length, sentence length, etc.

Additional categories of semantic features are used in languages such as English. Since the necessary resources and tools are not available for Arabic, we have not used these features.

In Chapter 3, we discussed the use of features derived from frequency lists and dictionaries. As mentioned in section 3.5, we have used our own dictionary of the 5,000 most frequent lemmas. On the basis of the different morphological information from the entries in this dictionary (lemma, PoS, frequency, etc.), we generated features for the documents in our corpora.

In total, we have developed 170 characteristics, grouped into ten categories as follows:

1. **Word length:** one of the traditional feature categories used in most previous work. For each text, we used the number of words, stems and characters. We also used the ratios number of characters per number of words and number of stems per number of words. The category contains a total of five characteristics;
2. **Sentence length:** we have also included average sentence length. We pointed out in Chapter 2 that both traditional and modern methods of measuring readability have included measures of sentence length. This category, made up of four characteristics, is expressed as the average number of words, stems and characters per sentence;
3. **Word class:** a list of four characteristics that assess the diversity of word classes in a text. We have used two word classes: open class and closed class. An open-class word is one whose grammatical category is one of infinite categories (such as nouns, verbs, etc.), whereas a closed-class word is one whose grammatical category is a finite list of words (such as pronouns);

4. **Vocabulary load:** a category based on the distribution of distinct and frequent lemmas in a text. It is composed of three characteristics:

(a) The number of distinct lemmas per text ;

(b) The number of frequent lemmas per text (lemmas appearing more than once) ;

(c) The ratio of frequent lemmas to total words in a text.

5. **The lemma/word relationship:** in our experiments we included four characteristics of the relationship between lemmas and words in a text. This is a category common to several previous studies;

6. **Word and lemma frequency:** for each text, we counted the number of lemmas in the frequency dictionary. We then divided this number by the total number of words in the document. We also introduced calculations on these variables (rank, ratio to stems, etc.) in order to provide a vocabulary study. Together, we have developed 17 characteristics;

7. **Ratios based on grammatical categories (PoS):** the category of ratios based on PoS encompasses 33 characteristics. It is inspired by Forsyth [Forsyth, 2014]. We have adapted it to match the PoS tags provided by MADAMIRA and the one provided by Alkhalil-Toolkit. In this category, we used the ratio between the individual occurrences of grammatical categories and the number of words in the document. To these ratios we have incorporated the ratios of PoS to word classes;

8. **Ambiguous lemmas:** a set of three characteristics that calculates the number of ambiguous lemmas. A lemma is said to be ambiguous if it obtains two or more distinct tags in the same text. We also used ratios in relation to words and lemmas in the text;

9. **Foreign words:** a single characteristic that represents the ratio of non-Arabic words to the total number of words in a text;

10. **Frequency based on grammatical categories:** the most voluminous category in this study with a total of 96 features. This category represents the ratios of individual frequent grammatical categories (which appear in the frequency dictionary) to words in the text.

A detailed list of these 170 characteristics is given in Appendix C.

5.3 Process adopted

Figure 5.1 shows the general process we have adopted to develop the predictive models of readability in L2. This process will be the same for most of the experiments we will present in this chapter, with adaptations in the different stages, i.e. changes in analysers, adaptation of characteristics, etc.

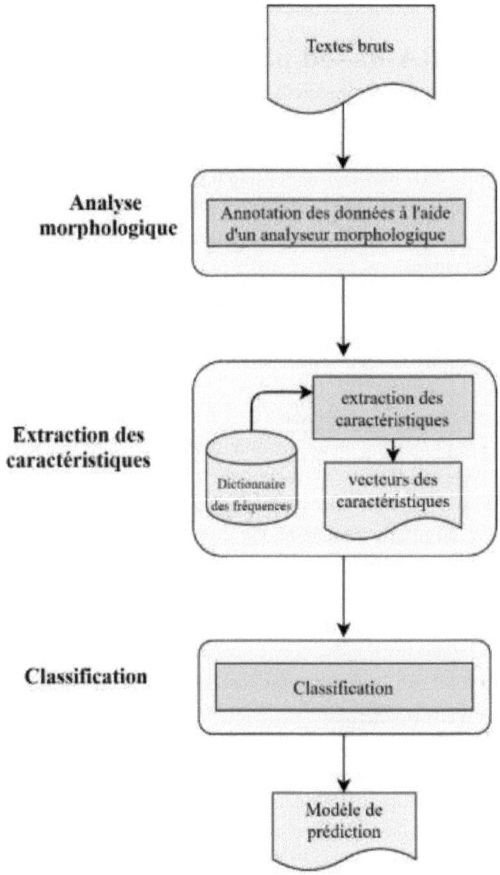

FIG. 5.1 : General process adapted to measure legibility in L2

To classify the texts in the three corpora, we use a three-stage process as follows (Figure 5.1):

1. **Morphological analysis**: the input for this phase is a text from one of the three corpora (GLOSS-Reading, GLOSS-Listening or Aljazeera-Learning). The result of this phase is a file (for each text) annotated with information such as the PoS, lemma, diacritic marks, etc ;
2. **Feature extraction**: in this stage, we extract and calculate all our features. To calculate the frequency-based features, we use the frequency dictionary we presented in Chapter 3. Finally, for each file in the corpus, we obtain a feature vector which we will use to prepare the input file for the classification phase;
3. **The classification phase**: based on WEKA, we apply the four classification algorithms J48, IBK, SMO and Random Forest, which we presented in detail in Chapter 2.

The aim of the process described above is to evaluate the influence of our characteristics on the prediction of the readability of L2.

In what follows, we describe the processes and results of a set of experiments carried out on the three corpora GLOSS-Reading, GLOSS-Listening and Aljazeera-Learning. These experiments are based on two parsers: MADAMIRA and Alkhalil-Toolkit.

To carry out these experiments we follow the process shown in Figure 5.1 above, with adaptations in the training and model generation phases. In the following sections, we will detail the different phases.

5.4 MADAMIRA-based predictive models

In this section, we will apply our predictive model generation process [Nassiri et al., 2018a] on our three corpora: GLOSS-Reading (**GR**), GLOSSListening (**GL**) and Aljazeera-Learning (**AL**). For the morphological annotation phase, we will use the MADAMIRA analyser. The process first consists of segmenting texts into sentences using the AraNLP library [Althobaiti et al., 2014]. The resulting file is then parsed with MADAMIRA to obtain an an- noted text containing the different morphological information such as PoS, lemma, stem, etc. For model generation, we will use the complete list of 170 features.

5.4.1 Using an 80/20% text split

This first experiment consists of generating a readability model on 80% of randomly selected data. The resulting model is then tested on the remaining 20%. This operation is carried out separately on the three corpora (GR, GL and AL) and is repeated for each of the four algorithms chosen, using five classes (1, 1+, 2, 2+ and 3).

During the corpus pre-processing phase, we eliminated all non-Arabic letters. As a result, the final corpora do not contain any foreign words (words written in non-Arabic letters). It was therefore pointless to include the 'Foreign words' category in the vector, as it would always be zero and would therefore give no information about the difficulty of the text. We therefore continued the work with only 169 characteristics.

We report the results of the experiments in terms of accuracy and F-measurement. Accuracy is calculated by the formula :

$$Exactitude = \frac{\text{nb des documents correctement prédits}}{\text{nb total des documents de l'ensemble du test}} \times 100. \qquad (5.1)$$

nb of documents correctly predicted

total no. of documents for the entire test^{X} ·

The precision of a class i is defined by the formula :

$$Prcision_i = \frac{\text{nb des documents correctement attribués à la classe i}}{\text{nb total des documents attribués à la classe i}} \qquad (5.2)$$

number of documents correctly assigned to class i

total number of documents assigned to class i

And it is generalized, for all the classes in the model, by the formula :

$$Prcision = \frac{\sum_{i=1}^{n} \text{Précision}_i}{n} \qquad (5.3)$$

Precisioni

prcision

The recall of a class i is defined by the formula :

$$Rappel_i = \frac{\text{nb des documents correctement attribués à la classe i}}{\text{nb des documents appartenant à la classe i}} \qquad (5.4)$$

Reminder$_i$ =

nb of documents correctly attributed to class i

nb of documents belonging to class i

And it is generalized, for all the classes in the model, by the formula :

$$Rappel = \frac{\sum_{i=1}^{n} \text{Rappel}_i}{n} \qquad (5.5)$$

Reminder

The F-measure is defined by the formula :

$$\text{F-mesure} = 2\times\frac{\text{Précision}\times\text{Rappel}}{\text{Précision}+\text{Rappel}} \quad (5.6)$$

PrecisionxReminder
Precision Rappel
The main difference between F-measure and accuracy is that accuracy can be used when the distribution of classes is similar, whereas F-measure is a better measure when there are unbalanced classes, as in our case.
Table 5.1 shows the results obtained when testing the models generated on data not encountered during the learning phase (the remaining 20% of the data) for GR, GL and AL. This first test is based on the first dictionary and five readability levels.

	GR		**GL**		**AL**	
	Accuracy	**F-measure**	**Accuracy**	**F-measure**	**Accuracy**	**F-measure**
J48	**61,81%**	**0,64**	44,44%	0,48	75,38%	**0,51**
IBK	45,45%	0,51	62,22%	0,62	69,23%	0,31
SMO	60,0%	0,60	**66,66%**	**0,66**	72,30%	0,39
RF	60,0%	0,61	62,22%	0,64	**80,0%**	0,44

Table 5.1: Test results for the 169 characteristics and MADAMIRA with the first five-class dictionary

We obtained a maximum accuracy value of 61.81% using the J48 algo- rithm for the GR corpus and an F-measure of 0.64. The GL corpus performed relatively better than GR with a maximum accuracy of 66.66% and an F-measure of 0.66 using the SMO algorithm. For the AL corpus, we obtained a maximum accuracy of 80% using the Random Forest (**RF**) algorithm, a performance which outperformed the other two corpora by more than 13%, but using the F-measure we obtained a value of 0.51 which is lower than the values of the other two corpora. This is due to the large imbalance of Aljazeera-Learning that we have already discussed in Chapter 4.
We have already mentioned that our three corpora suffer from an imbalance of data between the five classes. We therefore regenerated the models using three classes (easy, medium and difficult) instead of five, obtained by grouping classes "1" and "1+" in a single "easy" class, then classes "2+" and "3" in the "difficult" class. Class 2 represents the content of the 'medium' class. This division of the data into three classes is a scale adopted by several previous works [Forsyth, 2014] [Saddiki et al., 2015]. Table 5.2 shows the results obtained in this second test for
the three corpora. This test is also carried out on the basis of the first dictionary.

	GR		**GL**		**AL**	
	Accuracy	**F-measure**	**Accuracy**	**F-measure**	**Accuracy**	**F-measure**
J48	70,90%	0,73	62,22%	0,63	81,53%	0,74
IBK	63,63%	0,63	**73,33%**	0,72	75,38%	0,59
SMO	72,72%	0,72	**73,33%**	**0,75**	83,07%	0,75
RF	**74,54%**	**0,75**	**73,33%**	0,74	**86,15%**	**0,80**

Table 5.2: Test results for the 169 characteristics and MADAMIRA with the first dictionary on three classes

For the GR corpus, we obtained a maximum accuracy value of 74.54% using the RF algorithm while we obtained a maximum F-measure value of 0.75. The GL corpus showed a maximum accuracy of 73.33% using the IBK, SMO and RF algorithms respectively and obtained a maximum F-measure value of 0.75, so in terms of F-measure we can say that the two GLOSS corpora performed equally well. And for the AL corpus, we obtained a maximum accuracy of 86.15% with the RF algorithm and a maximum F-measure value of 0.80, which is much better than the value obtained using five classes.

Comparing the results of Tables 5.1 and 5.2, we obtained a gain in accuracy of more than 12% for the GR corpus and more than 6% for the GL and AL corpora. In terms of F-measurement, we obtained a gain of 0.29 for AL and 0.11 and 0.09 for GR and GL respectively.

Tables 5.3 and 5.4 show the results obtained by changing the first dictionary by the second dictionary (the one compiled from HindaouiCorpus). For five levels (Table 5.3), we obtained a maximum accuracy value of 63.63% using the RF algorithm for GR and an F-measure of 0.65 with the same algorithm, while we obtained a maximum accuracy value of 71.11% using the SMO algorithm for GL and an F-measure of 0.74. AL showed a maximum accuracy of 73.84% using the SMO and RF algorithms respectively but an F-measure of only 0.40. These results exceed the test with the first dictionary as expected with the exception of the AL corpus.

Finally, for the three levels (Table 5.4), we obtained a maximum accuracy value of 81.81% using the RF algorithm for GR and a maximum F-measure value of 0.82. For GL, we obtained a maximum accuracy value of 80.0% using the RF algorithm and a maximum F-measure of 0.81. For GR, we obtained a maximum accuracy value of 80.0% using the RF algorithm and a maximum F-measure of 0.81. For GL, we obtained a maximum accuracy value of 80.0% using the RF algorithm and a maximum F-measure value of 0.81. AL showed a maximum accuracy of 83.07% using the RF algorithm and a maximum F-measure of 0.76. As with the five-class classification, the results show the relevance of

	GR		GL		AL	
	Accuracy	**F-measure**	**Accuracy**	**F-measure**	**Accuracy**	**F-measure**
J48	54,54%	0,56	55,55%	0,55	67,69%	0,36
IBK	60,0%	0,60	62,22%	0,64	70,76%	0,31
SMO	58,18%	0,60	**71,11%**	**0,74**	**73,84%**	**0,40**
RF	**63,63%**	**0,65**	62,22%	0,64	**73,84%**	0,38

Table 5.3: Test results for the 169 characteristics and MADAMIRA with the second dictionary on five classes

the use of the second dictionary with the exception of the AL corpus.

	GR		GL		AL	
	Accuracy	**F-measure**	**Accuracy**	**F-measure**	**Accuracy**	**F-measure**
J48	69,09%	0,71	66,66%	0,68	80,0%	**0,76**
IBK	78,18%	0,81	64,44%	0,66	76,92%	0,59
SMO	76,36%	0,77	75,55%	0,75	81,53%	0,73
RF	**81,81%**	**0,82**	**80,0%**	**0,81**	**83,07%**	0,75

Table 5.4: Test results for the 169 characteristics and MADAMIRA with the second dictionary on three classes

To summarise this experiment, Figure 5.2 shows a comparison between the maximum accuracy values obtained with the three corpora using the two dictionaries. All the maximum values were obtained using the RF algorithm. Changing the first dictionary to the second improved the results of the prediction models. GR increased from 74.54% with the first dictionary to 81.81% with a gain of more than 7% in accuracy using the second dictionary, while GL increased from 73.33%

to 80% with a gain of more than 6% in accuracy. Only AL dropped from 86.15% to 83.07%, with a loss of around 3% in accuracy.

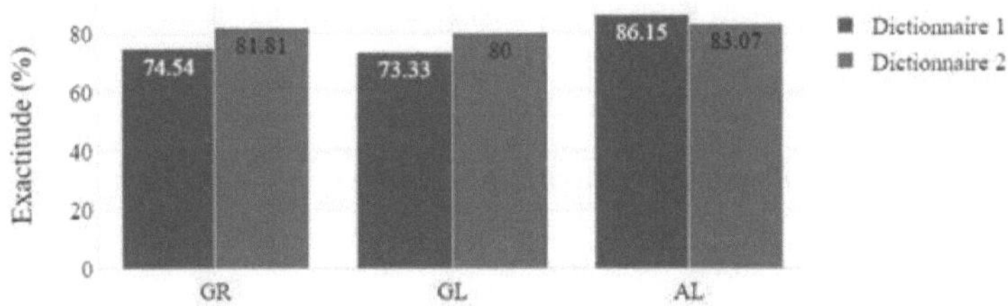

FIG. 5.2: Comparison of the accuracy values of the two dictionaries

For the F-measure, Figure 5.3 shows a comparison between the maximum values obtained with the three corpora in combination with the two dictionaries. For this measure too, the maximum values were obtained using the RF algorithm. The results obtained with the GR corpus using the second dictionary showed an improvement of 0.07 with an F-measure of 0.82 instead of 0.75, while GL increased from 0.75 to 0.81 with a gain of 0.06. As for accuracy, only AL went from an F-measure of 0.80 to 0.76, with a loss of 0.04.

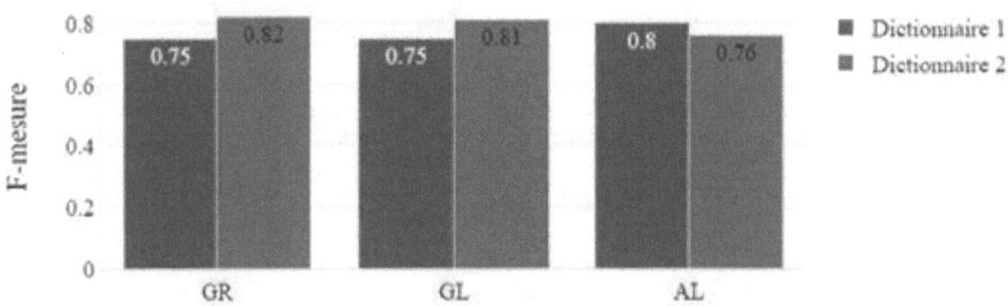

FIG. 5.3: Comparison of F-measurement values for the two dictionaries

5.4.2 Cross-validation

To better validate the results of the first experiment, we carried out a cross-validation. The process is as follows:

1. Each of the corpora used is divided into ten parts, each containing the same number of files of each class;
2. We apply the two steps of morphological annotation and feature extraction (see section 5.3) on the ten parts to obtain their vector files (one file per part);
3. We generate a model using nine vector files by applying the classification process (the last phase of the process we have adopted);
4. The models obtained are tested on the remaining part;
5. We repeat steps 3 and 4 nine times. At each iteration, we change the validation part so that all the parts are used for training and testing;
6. The final accuracy and F-measurement values are calculated as the averages of the 10 accuracy and F-measurement values from the 10 tests.

This process is repeated for the four algorithms used and each algorithm is applied on five and three levels (for the three corpora used: AL, GR and GL). The results of this experiment are also obtained using the set containing the 169 characteristics and they will be relatively inferior to the first experiment, since here an average of 10 tests is calculated.

Table 5.5 shows the results of this experiment using the first dictionary and five classes. GR provided a maximum accuracy of 61.25%, with a loss of 0.56% compared to the first experiment, and an F-measure of 0.60. Under the same conditions, AL showed an increase of 0.06% while GL decreased by more than 7% with a maximum accuracy of 59.47% instead of 66.66% in the first experiment and an F-measure of 0.57.

	GR		GL		AL	
	Accuracy	**F-measure**	**Accuracy**	**F-measure**	**Accuracy**	**F-measure**
J48	47,23%	0,47	48,45%	0,48	71,65%	0,71
IBK	46,86%	0,44	50,22%	0,49	76,32%	0,68
SMO	53,87%	0,53	55,94%	0,55	76,63%	**0,74**
RF	**61,25%**	**0,60**	**59,47%**	**0,57**	**80,06%**	0,73

Table 5.5: Results of cross-validation with the first dictionary and five classes

For the three classes, we obtained a maximum accuracy of 74.53% for GR, 73.12% for GL and 85.66% for AL using three levels giving a decrease of 0.01%, 0.21% and 0.49% for GR, GL and AL respectively as shown in Table 5.6. We also obtained an F-measure of 0.74, 0.73 and 0.84 for GR, GL and AL respectively. Given that the decreases do not exceed 1%, with the exception of GL in five classes, we can confirm the results of the first experiment (those obtained with the 80/20% of the data).

	GR		GL		AL	
	Accuracy	**F-measure**	**Accuracy**	**F-measure**	**Accuracy**	**F-measure**
J48	67,52%	0,67	62,99%	0,63	80,99%	0,80
IBK	57,19%	0,57	59,91%	0,59	81,61%	0,78
SMO	69,37%	0,69	67,84%	0,68	82,24%	0,80
RF	**74,53%**	**0,74**	**73,12%**	**0,73**	**85,66%**	**0,84**

Table 5.6: Cross-validation results with the first dictionary and three classes

We repeated the same experiments, replacing the first dictionary with the second. Table 5.7 shows the results obtained in this case using five classes. We obtained a maximum accuracy of 61.25% for GR, 61.23% for GL and 79.43% for AL. For the F-measure we obtained a value of 0.60 for GR and GL respectively, while for AL we obtained an F-measure of 0.72.

Table 5.8 shows the results obtained under the same conditions using three classes instead of five. We obtained a maximum accuracy of 78.96% for

	GR		GL		AL	
	Accuracy	**F-measure**	**Accuracy**	**F-measure**	**Accuracy**	**F-measure**
J48	47,97%	0,47	47,57%	0,47	71,02%	0,70
IBK	52,02%	0,50	53,30%	0,52	76,01%	0,63
SMO	55,35%	0,54	**61,23%**	**0,60**	74,14%	0,71
RF	**61,25%**	**0,60**	56,82%	0,54	**79,43%**	**0,72**

Table 5.7: Results of cross-validation with the second dictionary and five classes

GR, 73.12% for GL and 85.98% for AL. For the F-measurement we obtained a value of 0.78, 0.73 and 0.84 for GR, GL and AL respectively.

	GR		GL		AL	
	Accuracy	**F-measure**	**Accuracy**	**F-measure**	**Accuracy**	**F-measure**

J48	63,09%	0,63	62,55%	0,62	82,24%	0,81
IBK	68,26%	0,68	63,87%	0,63	81,93%	0,81
SMO	69,74%	0,69	67,84%	0,67	82,86%	0,80
RF	**78,96%**	**0,78**	**73,12%**	**0,73**	**85,98%**	**0,84**

Table 5.8: Results of cross-validation with the second dictionary and three classes

Figure 5.4 shows a comparison of the maximum accuracy values obtained in the cross-validation experiments using the two dictionaries and three classes. We note that the second dictionary performed better than the first dictionary for the GR corpus, with an accuracy of 78.96% instead of 74.53%. For the GL corpus, we obtained the same accuracy of 73.12% with both dictionaries, while AL showed an improvement of 0.32% by using the second dictionary instead of the first.

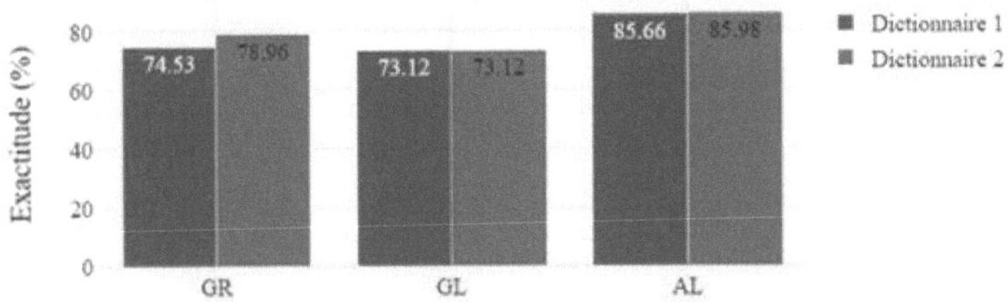

FIG. 5.4 : Comparison of cross-validation accuracy values for the two dictionaries

The results illustrated in Figure 5.5 show a comparison of the maximum F-measure values obtained in the cross-validation experiments using the two dictionaries and three classes. The second dictionary performed better than the first dictionary for the GR corpus, with a value of 0.78 instead of 0.74. We obtained an F-measure value equal to 0.73 and 0.84 for the GL and AL corpora respectively, using both dictionaries.

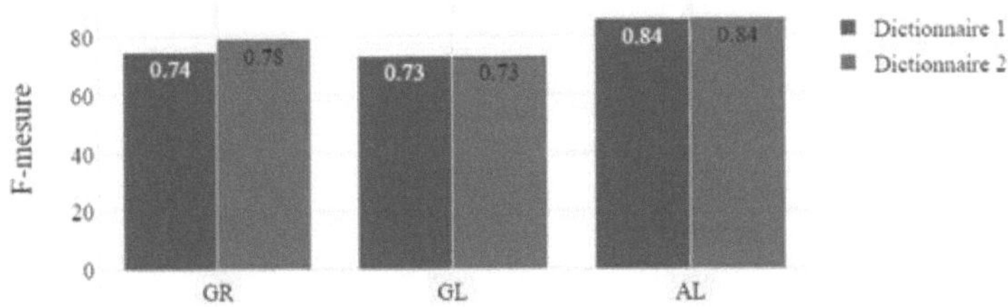

FIG. 5.5 : Comparison of cross-validation F-measure values for the two dictionaries

From the results of the two sections (5.4.1 and 5.4.2) we can conclude that the second dictionary performs better than the first. We will therefore continue the rest of the experiments in this thesis with a single frequency dictionary (the second dictionary compiled from *HindaouiCorpus*) and with an 80/20% distribution of the data.

5.5 Models based on Alkhalil-Toolkit

The experiments, which we will present in this section, are carried out using the same process as the previous section but replacing the MADAMIRA parser with Alkhalil-Toolkit [Nassiri et al., 2018b]. As the two analysers do not use the same tags (Alkhalil-Toolkit uses 27 tags whereas MADAMIRA uses 34 tags), we proceeded to a readaptation of the list of characteristics. This allowed us to reduce the number of characteristics from 169 to 137. Table 5.9 shows the new breakdown into categories.

Table 5.10 shows the correspondence between the tags of the two analysers used. The differences essentially concern the categories: noun, adjective, adverb, particle and conjunction. In addition to these differences, the characteristic "*ratio of punctuation to total words*" is ignored, since Alkhalil-Toolkit ignores punctuation at the time of tagging.

In what follows, we will present two series of experiments. One series :

1. Using the three corpora independently;
2. By merging the three corpora.

Category	**Old size**	**New size**
Frequencies based on PoS	96	71
Ratios between lemma PoS and words	33	26
Word and lemma sequences	17	17
Word to word ratio	4	4
Average word length	5	5
Vocabulary load	3	3
Word classes	4	4
Average sentence length	4	4
Ambiguity	3	3
Total	**169**	**137**

Table 5.9: Breakdown of Alkhalil-Toolkit features by category

category	**MADAMIRA**	**Alkhalil-Toolkit**
Name	noun noun_num noun_quant	No
Adjective	adj adj_num	Sifa
Adverb	adv adv_rel	Dz
Particle	part part_focus part_interrog part_verb	PaNs PNa CJ
Conjunction	conj conj_sub	Co

Table 5.10: Correspondence between MADAMIRA and Alkhalil-Toolkit tags

5.5.1 Using the three corpora independently

Table 5.11 shows the results of this first experiment with a five-level classification. For AL, we obtained a maximum accuracy value of 81.53% but with an F-measure of only 0.46. For GR, we obtained 63.63% as the maximum accuracy and 0.61 as the F-measure. For GR, we obtained 63.63% as maximum accuracy and 0.61 as F-measure. GL provided 55.55% maximum accuracy and 0.47 F-measure using the RF algorithm. These results are better than the first experiment, with the exception of the GL corpus, which fell from 71.11% to 55.55%.

	GR		GL		AL	
	Accuracy	F-measure	Accuracy	F-measure	Accuracy	F-measure
J48	50,90%	0,53	53,33%	**0,56**	70,76%	0,34
IBK	52,72%	0,53	42,22%	0,41	67,69%	**0,56**
SMO	60,0%	0,61	**55,55%**	0,54	80,0%	0,44
RF	**63,63%**	**0,61**	**55,55%**	0,47	**81,53%**	0,46

Table 5.11: Results of Alkhalil-Toolkit tests on five classes

	GR		GL		AL	
	Accuracy	F-measure	Accuracy	F-measure	Accuracy	F-measure
J48	61,81%	0,65	71,11%	0,73	78,46%	0,70
IBK	67,27%	0,68	62,22%	0,58	70,76%	0,61
SMO	**81,81%**	**0,82**	**75,55%**	0,74	**87,69%**	**0,82**
RF	80,0%	0,81	**75,55%**	**0,75**	**87,69%**	**0,82**

Table 5.12: Results of Alkhalil-Toolkit tests on three classes

For three levels, the results presented in Table 5.12 illustrate that GR achieves a maximum accuracy of 81.81% with the SMO algorithm and a maximum F-measure of 0.82. GL demonstrated an accuracy of 75.55% using both the SMO and RF algorithms and an F-measure of 0.75, while AL provided 87.69% as the maximum accuracy using both the SMO and RF algorithms in addition to an F-measure of 0.82. Once again, the results are better than those obtained with MADAMIRA, with the exception of the GL corpus, which fell from 80% to 75.55%.

Using Alkhalil-Toolkit instead of MADAMIRA with the AL corpus increased the maximum accuracy from 83.07% to 87.5%, which leads us to conclude that the AL corpus performs better with Alkhalil-Toolkit than with MADAMIRA.

5.5.2 Merging the three corpora

After presenting the performance of each corpus independently in the previous experiments, one question that arose was why not merge the three corpora? We therefore merged the three corpora and repeated the previous experiments on the new corpus. Table 5.13 shows the distribution by level of the texts in the new corpus. Table 5.14 shows the results of these experiments on five and three classes.

	Number of texts	Number of sentences	Number of words
1	88	3 201	16 023
1+	267	1 719	29 327
2	213	2 550	53 244
2+	156	2 851	59 914
3	92	2 132	42 074
Total	**816**	**12 453**	**200 582**

Table 5.13: Level distribution of the merged corpus

	5 classes		3 classes	
	Accuracy	F-measure	Accuracy	F-measure
J48	50,30%	0,49	66,66%	0,63
IBK	45,45%	0,40	63,03%	0,61
SMO	60,0%	0,56	**77,57%**	**0,75**
RF	**67,27%**	**0,65**	76,36%	0,72

Table 5.14: Test results for the merged corpus

For five classes, we obtained a maximum accuracy of 67.27% and an F-measure of 0.65 using the RF algorithm. For three classes, we obtained a maximum accuracy of 77.57% and an F-measure of 0.75 using the SMO algorithm. The results of these experiments are inferior to the values obtained in the previous experiments. This can be justified by the fact that the accuracy of the worst-performing corpus automatically affects that of the other corpora. It should also be noted that the three corpora are relatively different in terms of :

1. Their types: the GR corpus is a reading corpus unlike the GL which is a listening corpus;
2. Their sources: the GLOSS corpus and the AL corpus come from different sources.

In the rest of the thesis, we will work with the three corpora independently morphologically annotated with Alkhalil-Toolkit.

5.6 Reducing the size of text vectors

The selection and quality of the characteristics representing each model have an influence on the success of the subsequent classification. During the feature extraction phase, new features can be derived from the original features to increase the efficiency of the classifier and enable greater accuracy. Although this is useful for data visualisation and classification efficiency, it does not necessarily reduce the number of features to be measured, since each new feature can be a linear combination of other features in the original vector.

In this section, we present an approach to feature reduction based on two assumptions:

1. Derived characteristics and original characteristics can sometimes carry the same information. This was the subject of an initial experiment to decide whether to keep only the original characteristics or both;
2. Some characteristics are more relevant than others. The second experiment aims to evaluate the impact of using the best predictors.

5.6.1 Omission of derived characteristics

The set of 137 characteristics obtained from the previous experiment includes a set of ratios whose component characteristics are also part of the vector. We will begin by eliminating these ratios to see the effect of this elimination. Table 5.15 lists the eliminated ratios and their component characteristics (we use the abbreviations in Appendix C).

It should also be noted that the "Word/word ratio" category has been completely ignored, as it is made up of ratios only. The rest of the experiments are carried out using only eight categories of characteristics instead of nine.

The omission of these ratios gave us a new list of 117 characteristics instead of 137. The distribution of the new characteristics by category is shown in Table 5.16.

Figure 5.6 shows the maximum accuracy values obtained by performing the tests.

Ratio	Component features
SL2	WL1 / SL1
SL3	WL5 / SL1
SL4	WL4 / SL1
WL2	WL4 / WL1
WL3	WL5 / WL1
WC2	WC1 / WL1
WC4	WC3 / WL1
AMb2	AMb1 / WL1
AMb3	AMb1 / VL1
VL3	VL2 / WL1
TTPR4	TTPR28 / WL1
TTPR8	TTPR27 / WL1
TTPR10	TTPR29 / WL1
TTPR22	TTPR31 / WL1

Table 5.15: List of some ratios

Category	Old size	New size
Frequencies based on PoS	71	71
Ratios between lemma PoS and words	26	22
Word and lemma sequences	17	15
Word to word ratio	4	0
Average word length	5	3
Vocabulary load	3	2
Word classes	4	2
Average sentence length	4	1
Ambiguity	3	1
Total	**137**	**117**

Table 5.16: Breakdown of characteristics by category after omission of ratios

on three classes. For the AL corpus, we obtained a maximum accuracy value of 86.69%, a value identical to that obtained before the ratios were omitted. For the GL corpus, all 117 predictors made it possible to obtain an accuracy value of 82.22% instead of 75.55%, a gain of more than 6%. Only the GR corpus showed a decrease of 1.81%, with an accuracy of 80% instead of 81.81%.

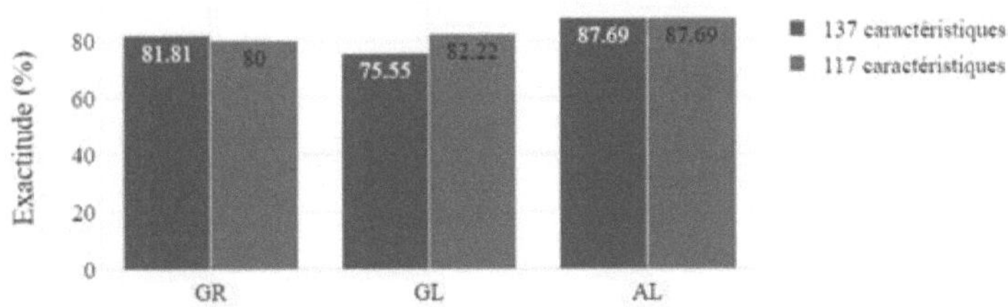

FIG. 5.6 : Accuracy results after omitting ratios using three classes

Figure 5.7 shows the maximum F-measure values obtained for three classes. The AL corpus retained the same value of 0.82 for both sets of characteristics, while the GR corpus showed a decrease of 0.01 and GL an increase of 0.07 after the ratios were omitted.

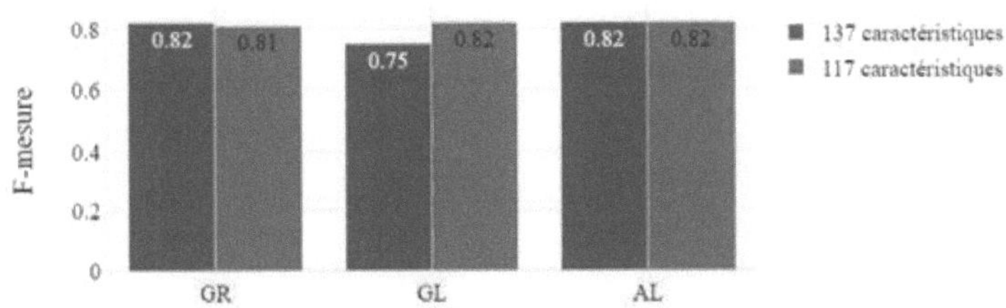

FIG. 5.7 : F-measurement results after omission of ratios using three classes

The results of the two experiments show that we have a gain in accuracy and F-measurement for the GL corpus and stable values for the AL corpus, whereas we have a slight loss with the GR corpus. This confirms the hypothesis concerning the usefulness of keeping the original characteristics and ignoring the derivatives.

5.6.2 Selecting the best predictors

The main objective of this experiment is to determine the most relevant characteristics and see their impact on predicting legibility. To do this, we followed the process outlined below:

1. For each of the eight categories of characteristics obtained in the previous experiments, we generated a vector file;
2. For each file generated, we carried out an automatic selection of characteristics with WEKA, using the "CfsSubsetEval" method [Hall, 2000]. This method evaluates the value of a subset of attributes by considering the individual predictive capacity of each characteristic and the degree of redundancy between them. Subsets of characteristics that are strongly correlated with the class while having low intercorrelation are preferred. We have combined this method with the "BestFirst" search method [Korf, 1993], which searches the space for subsets of attributes. It starts with the empty set of attributes and searches forwards, or with the complete set of attributes and searches backwards, or at any point and searches in both directions (considering all possible additions and deletions of a single attribute at a given point);
3. We selected the best characteristics obtained in each category and combined them to obtain a new WEKA input file containing 70 characteristics;
4. Finally, we applied the process used previously (see section 5.3), with the new set of characteristics on three classes. We ran the test on the three corpora, using 80% of the data for training and 20% for testing.

Table 5.17 shows the distribution of this new set of characteristics by category. We have kept the eight categories with a total of 70 characteristics instead of the original 170.

Category	**Old size**	**New size**
Frequencies based on PoS	71	37
Ratios between lemma PoS and words	22	15
Word and lemma sequences	15	10
Average word length	3	3
Vocabulary load	2	2
Word classes	2	1
Average sentence length	1	1
Ambiguity	1	1
Total	**117**	**70**

Table 5.17: Classification of characteristics after selection of the best predictors

Figure 5.8 shows the maximum accuracy values obtained using this new set of predictors. For the AL corpus, we obtained a maximum accuracy value of 84.61% instead of 87.69%, while for the GR corpus we obtained a maximum accuracy value of 81.81% instead of 80%, unlike the GL corpus, for which we obtained a maximum accuracy value of 75.55% instead of 82.22%.

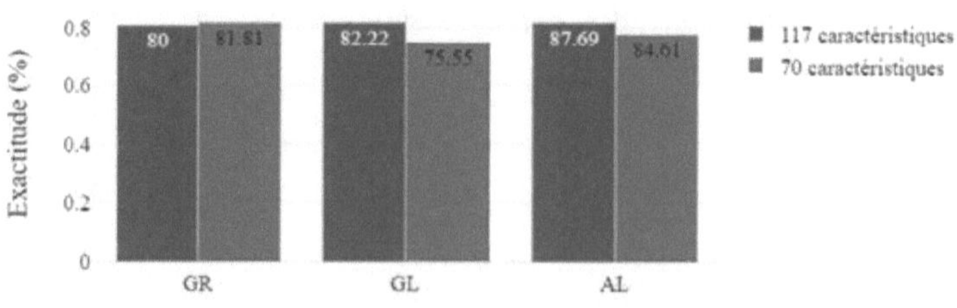

FIG. 5.8: Accuracy results after selection of the best predictors using three classes

The results in terms of F-measure are shown in Figure 5.9. For AL, we obtained an F-measure value of 0.78, while for the GR corpus we obtained a value of 0.82, compared with 0.75 as the F-measure for the GL corpus.

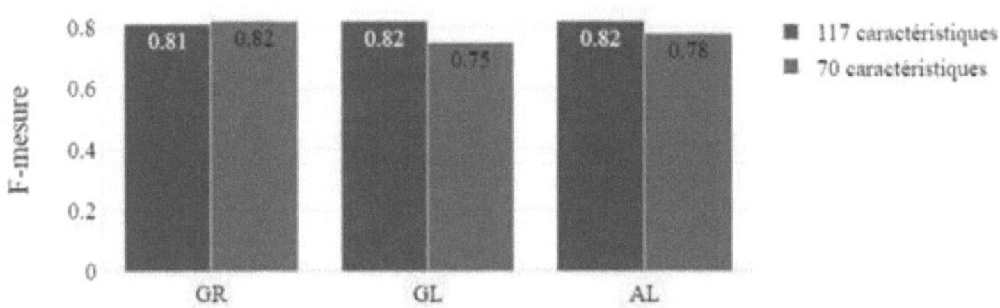

FIG. 5.9 : F-measurement results after selection of the best predictors using three classes

Comparing the slight decrease in accuracy and F-measurement from 170 features to just 70, shows that the final set of 70 features is the most significant of all the predictors we collected.
It should be noted that all results were obtained using data equilibrium sets. In the next section, we will give techniques to overcome this problem.

5.7 Data rebalancing

In this section, we'll look at how to manage a set of desequilibrated data.
Table 5.18 shows the statistics for the three corpora used. It should be noted that class 2 is in the majority for the GR and GL corpora, whereas class 1+ is in the majority for the AL corpus.

Level	GR	GL	AL
1	34	43	12
1+	29	18	220
2	95	65	54
2+	68	62	27
3	45	39	8
Total	**271**	**227**	**321**

Table 5.18: Statistics on the corpora used

Most ML algorithms tend to favour the majority class. To favour the other classes as well, there are techniques such as Under-Sampling and Over-Sampling [Liu, 2004]. Over-sampling and under-sampling are used to modify unequal classes of data in order to create balanced data sets.
Oversampling is used, when the amount of data collected is insufficient, to reproduce the results in order to obtain a more balanced amount of data in the training. Among the most popular oversampling techniques is the Synthetic Minority Over-sampling Technique (**SMOTE**) [Chawla et al., 2002] (see Appendix D), an approach in which the minority class is oversampled by creating 'synthetic' examples obtained by randomly sampling the characteristics of the occurrences of this class. We used this technique to balance our data and check its impact on the performance of our predictive models. The process adopted during this experiment is as follows:

- We apply our annotation and feature vector extraction process to all the data in the three corpora;
- For each corpus we generate a file containing the vectors representing the texts in the corpus;
- Using the Random Forest algorithm implemented in the Python "**scikit-learn** [1]" library, we perform an initial classification using an 80/20% distribution of the vectors generated;
- The accuracy results by level of this first classification are shown in Table 5.19 ;

	GR	GL	AL
1	83,33%	77,77%	-
1+	66,66%	16,66%	95,65%

2	80%	75%	66,66%
2+	25%	45,45%	88,88%
3	66,66%	50%	0%
Total	**60%**	**56,52%**	**89,23%**

Table 5.19: Results of tests on unbalanced data

- Then, we apply the SMOTE technique on the training vectors to balance them and we obtain a new distribution of the vectors. For the AL corpus, the "1+" class is the majority class with a total of 166 vectors. After SMOTE, all the classes in AL will have the same total (166 vectors);
- The accuracy results by level, obtained using the balanced data, are presented in Table 5.20.

	GR	GL	AL
1	83,33%	88,88%	-
1 +	87,5%	33,33%	97,82%
2	60%	75%	100%
2+	31,25%	45,45%	100%
3	77,77%	62,5%	100%
Total	**60%**	**63,04%**	**98,46**

Table 5.20: Results of tests on data after oversampling

Comparing the results of tables 5.19 and 5.20, we can conclude that the use of rebalancing techniques has improved the classification results, both in terms of total accuracy and the accuracy of each level independently.

1. https://scikit-learn.org (last visited 10/11/2020)

5.8 Comparison with the state of the art

Most of the work reported in the state of the art is carried out on the GLOSSReading corpus using three classes and using the same algorithms as we have used. In Figure 5.10, we compare the maximum accuracy of our work with that of the state of the art. Under the same conditions, the maximum accuracy value was reported by [Saddiki et al., 2015] and is 73.31%. In our case, we reported a maximum accuracy value of 81.81%.

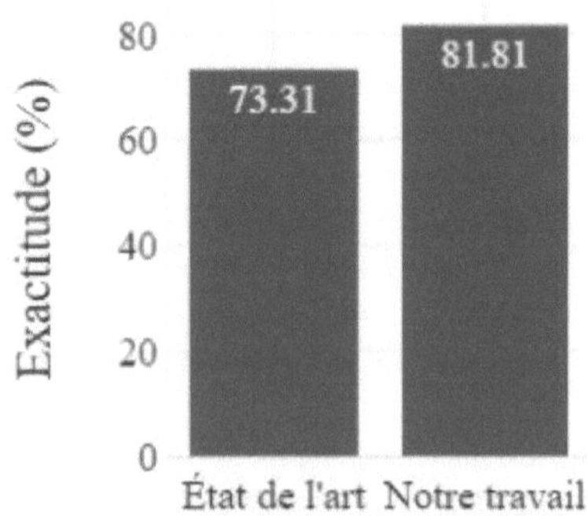

FIG. 5.10: Comparison of the maximum accuracy value with the state of the art value

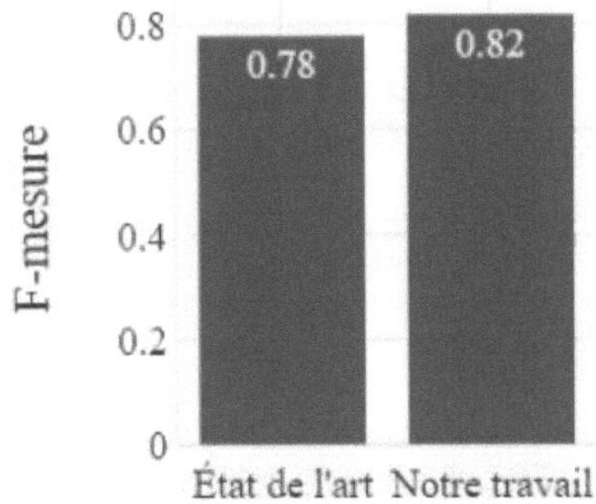

FIG. 5.11: Comparison of the value of the maximum F-measurement with that of the state of the art

Again using GLOSS with three classes, [Forsyth, 2014] reported the maximum state-of-the-art F-measure which is equal to 0.78. As shown in Figure 5.11, we reported an F-measure of 0.82 under the same conditions.

5.9 Conclusion

In this chapter, we have presented a set of experiments that use ML techniques to predict the readability of texts intended for L2 learners. We trained and tested our models using the Aljazeera-Learning (AL), GLOSS-Reading (GR) and GLOSS-Listening (GL) corpora.

The first objective is to evaluate the impact of the set of collected characteristics on the prediction of the readability of L2. The second objective is to reduce the set of features used in the prediction process while maintaining or increasing the performance obtained with the initial set of features. In the first experiments reported, we generated the prediction models on 80% of the data, selected at random. The generated models were then tested on the remaining 20%. We then carried out a cross-validation experiment based on 10 samples in order to validate the results of the first classification.

The first experiment was based on the extraction of 169 characteristics and was carried out using MADAMIRA as the morphological analyser. The model tests reached a maximum accuracy of 81.81% with GR and an F-measure of 0.82. 80% and 0.81 are the accuracy and F-measure values obtained with GL, while 83.07% and 0.76 are obtained with AL using the Random Forest algorithm, three classes and the second dictionary introduced in Chapter 3. The use of cross-validation under these same conditions resulted in maximum accuracy of 78.96%, 73.12% and 85.98% and F-measurements of 0.78, 0.73 and 0.84 for GR, GL and AL respectively.

Changing the MADAMIRA parser to Alkhalil-Toolkit and using the second dictionary reduced the number of features from 169 to 137 after adapting the predictors to all the parser tags. We obtained maximum accuracy values of 81.81%, 75.55% and 87.69% for GR, GL and AL respectively using the SMO algorithm and three classes. For the F-measure, we obtained 0.82 for GR and AL, and 0.75 for the GL corpus.

We have also reported the results of tests which consisted of ignoring a number of characteristics which showed poor performance. The results of these experiments show that the ignored features do not significantly influence the classification process. This is promising because, if we want to use our model to make suggestions to instructors about which features to take into account when choosing or creating texts for L2 learners, it is better to use a smaller set of features.

Finally, we reported the results of the development of a prediction model based on data that we had re-equilibrated. The results of this last experiment proved that oversampling improves the prediction results of our models.

Chapter 6

Measuring readability in L1

6.1 Introduction

The process of teaching a language during the primary school years requires materials that are adapted to the reading level and skills of the pupils. If the material presented to a reader is easy to read and contains clear and orderly ideas, it is more likely that the learner's enthusiasm for reading will increase. Hence the need to choose the right level of difficulty for the texts presented to readers.

As we have already mentioned, current readability measurement methods use ML to predict the difficulty level of a given text. For Arabic, most of the work is dedicated to L2. On the other hand, little research is devoted to L1.

In this chapter, we have used the MoSAR corpus dedicated to L1 learners and annotated with six levels of difficulty. We have also used a readability measurement approach based on characteristics inspired by our work on L2 and which we have adapted for L1. This approach is a combination of classical and non-classical characteristics. The aim is to evaluate the performance of these features in predicting L1 readability. We will describe and discuss the process followed, the features used and the results obtained.

6.2 Applying the characteristics of L2 to L1

During our experiments on L2 we demonstrated that the ratio characteristics do not affect the prediction process because the same information is carried by the original predictors. We will begin work on L1 with this reduced set of 117 characteristics obtained by ignoring the ratios. We cannot start the experiments with the final set of 70 features because these are obtained using an approach linked to the corpora used. The first experiment consists mainly of evaluating the impact of applying the 117 characteristics on the prediction of readability in L1. Table 6.1 shows the results obtained using the MoSAR corpus in order to evaluate the impact of the features on this corpus. We obtained a maximum accuracy of 63.33% using RF but a maximum F-measure of only 0.58.

	Accuracy	F-measure
J48	55%	0,50
IBK	36,66%	0,36
SMO	47,5%	0,44
RF	**63,33%**	**0,58**

Table 6.1: Test results for 117 characteristics on MoSAR using six levels

Most of the work reported in the state of the art uses three levels: easy, medium and difficult. To use these three classes, we have re-annotated the levels of the MoSAR corpus as follows:

- Easy level: combines levels 1 and 2 ;
- Medium level: combines levels 3 and 4 ;
- Difficult level: combines levels 5 and 6.

The final experiment reported in Table 6.2 involves prediction using only three classes. The maximum accuracy obtained is 71.66% with an F-measure of 0.71 using the RF algorithm.

	Accuracy	F-measure
J48	65,0%	0,64
IBK	54,16%	0,54

SMO	60,83%	0,61
RF	**71,66%**	**0,71**

Table 6.2: Test results for 117 characteristics on MoSAR using three levels

The results obtained allow us to conclude that the 117 predictors of L2 have a significant impact on L1. To improve these results, we adopted two strategies:

1. Eliminate features that reduce accuracy;
2. Incorporate other features.

6.3 Selecting the best predictors

As with L2, the aim of this experiment is to determine the best-performing characteristics among the 117. As indicated in section 5.6.2, the process consists of :

1. Generate vectors for each category of characteristics ;
2. Select the best predictors for each category;
3. Finally, combine the best characteristics in a single vector to use it as a new input for the classification phase.

The application of this process resulted in a list of 37 characteristics, grouped by categories as shown in Table 6.3. As shown in Figures 6.1 and 6.2, the results obtained with this new list are better than with the old list. The results are obtained using the RF algorithm.

Category	**Old size**	**New size**
Frequencies based on PoS	71	17
Ratios between lemma PoS and words	22	8
Word and lemma sequences	15	4
Average word length	3	3
Vocabulary load	2	2
Word classes	2	1
Average sentence length	1	1
Ambiguity	1	1
Total	**117**	**37**

Table 6.3: Breakdown by category of best predictors in L1

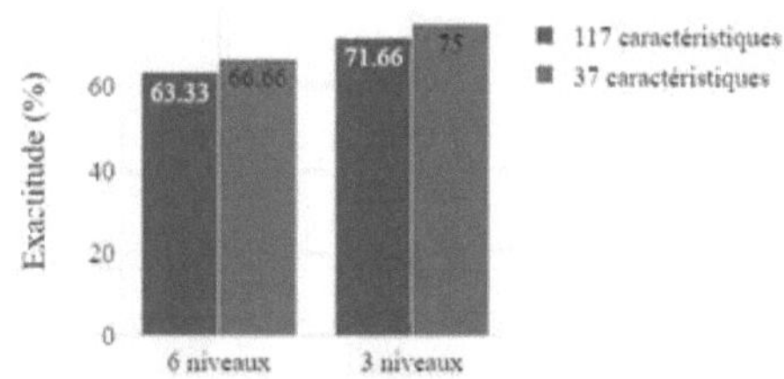

Fig. 6.1: Maximum accuracy obtained after selecting the best predictors in L1

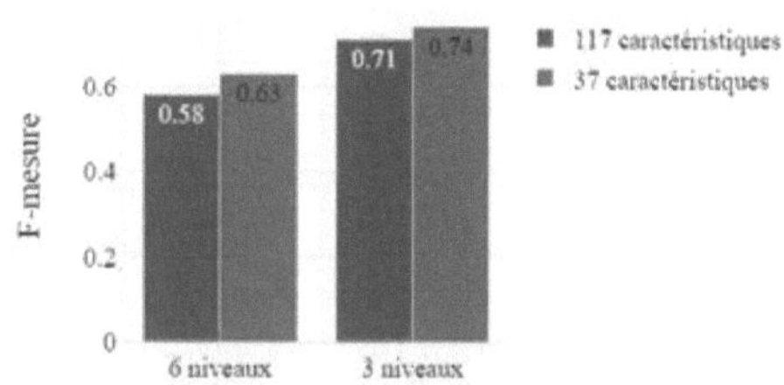

Fig. 6.2: Maximum F-measures obtained after selecting the best predictors in L1

6.4 Incorporating vocabulary skills

There is a strong link between vocabulary knowledge and the readability of texts. Vocabulary knowledge has always been considered to be the main indicator of the difficulty of a text. The procedures used to assess the vocabulary factor vary, including syllable counts, word frequency counts, and so on. In general, counts of 'easy' or 'difficult' words in a text are very important in detecting whether a text is easy or difficult. Other research states that the vocabulary known by the reader is important [Cavalli-Sforza et al., 2014].

In order to verify this hypothesis, we will introduce the "vocabulary content" family into our tests. The approach is based on a division of the vocabulary of a text into what is "known" and what is "target". A vocabulary is :

- **Target**, if it is intended for learning at the current level of competence, that to which the text belongs;
- **Known**, if it has already been learned before this level of competence.

A text is suitable for a level of study if it contains a certain proportion of words targeted by that level and enough words that are easily recognisable by the learner, i.e. known. We conducted two experiments based on this approach, the first using word-based lexicons and the second using lemma-based lexicons.

The process of this experiment consists of :

1. Develop a vocabulary lexicon for each of the six main levels. The lexicon for each level contains the new words/lemmes for that level, ignoring those from previous levels;
2. For each text in the corpus, add to the vector of the 37 best characteristics selected, six characteristics each corresponding to the number of words/lemmas known in a given level (the number of words/lemas in the text which belong to the lexicons of the previous levels);
3. For each text in the corpus, add to the new vector obtained in the second step, six other characteristics, each corresponding to the number of target words/lemmas in a given level (the number of words/lemas in the text that belong to the lexicon of the current level and that are not included in the lexicons of the previous levels);
4. Use the new vector, of size 49, to develop new prediction models.

The models are developed using the four learning algorithms. For the three-level test, the vector size will be 43, as we will be using three features from the known vocabulary and three from the target vocabulary.

Table 6.4 shows the sizes of the lexicons for each level of study. These lexicons are generated using the corpus training data (the 80%).

Level	Size of word lexicon	Size of the lexicon of lemmas
1	1 437	779
2	4 665	2 374
3	2 789	1 359
4	6 463	2 999
5	4 446	2 051
6	2 582	1 077

Table 6.4: Size of MoSAR lexicons

The best results in this experiment were obtained using the IBK algorithm, unlike the 37-characteristics experiment which gave the best values using the RF algorithm. Figure 6.3 shows the results of incorporating this new category, based on words, in terms of accuracy. For the results based on the six primary levels and the three levels, we obtained a maximum accuracy of

57.49% and 50.83% respectively, very low values compared to the values of the previous experiment.

Figure 6.4 shows the best results in terms of F-measurement. For the six levels, we obtained a maximum value of 0.55 instead of 0.63. Using three levels gave a maximum value of 0.56 instead of 0.74.

Figure 6.5 shows the accuracy results obtained by repeating the same experiment with a change from word lexicons to lemma lexicons. The use of the lemma-based lexicon instead of the word-based lexicon allowed us to obtain a better accuracy.

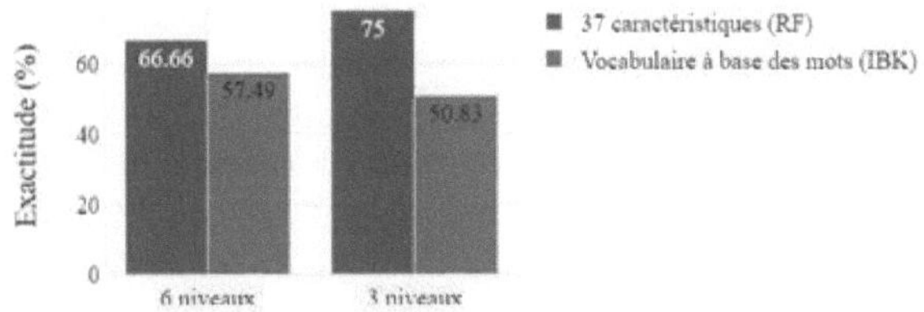

Fig. 6.3: Maximum accuracies obtained using word-based vocabulary mastery

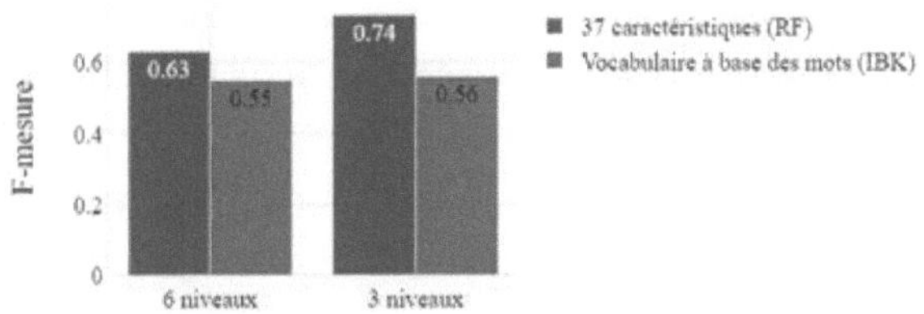

Fig. 6.4: Maximum F-measurements obtained using word-based vocabulary control

For the six levels, the maximum accuracy was 68.33%, a value that exceeds those obtained in all previous experiments on the six levels. The three levels reported a maximum accuracy of 50.83%, as for the word-based lexicon.

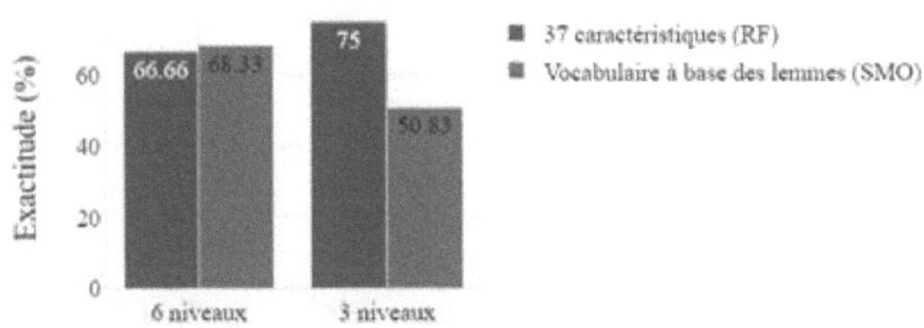

Fig. 6.5: Maximum accuracies obtained using lemma-based vocabulary control

For the F-measurement, we obtained a maximum value of 0.66 and 0.53 respectively for six and three levels (see Figure 6.6).

The aim of this experiment was to verify the hypothesis of the impact of vocabulary mastery on the difficulty of comprehending a text. This family of characteristics produced good results using the six primary levels (without grouping levels and lexicons), with a gain of 1.33% in accuracy and 0.03 in F-measurement compared with all the experiments we carried out.

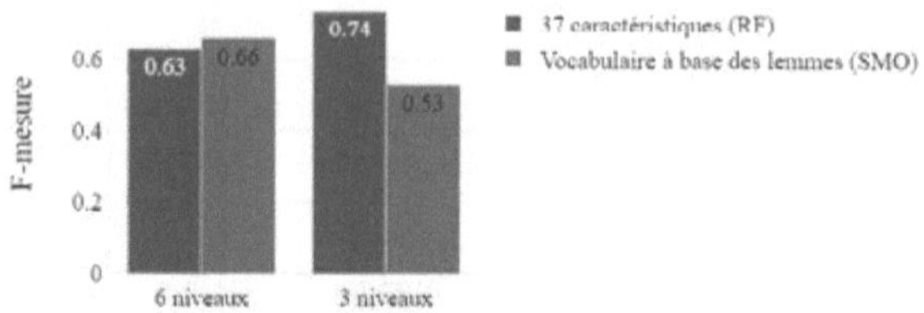

Fig. 6.6: Maximum F-measures obtained using lemma-based vocabulary control

6.5 Incorporating perplexity scores

Language Models (LMs) are also a category of features that have been applied to readability measurement for several years. These LMs offer many advantages in terms of computation, but also require huge text corpora for parameter estimation. In addition, the texts must accurately reflect the user's language in the statistical sense. Estimating a language model on a non-representative sample seriously affects the performance of predictive models.

The process of this experiment consists of :

1. Build a bi-gram statistical language model for each readability level. In this step we generate six LMs for the six levels and three LMs for the three levels. All these LMs are developed using the training data;
2. Using shaped models to calculate perplexity scores. To do this, we calculate a perplexity score for each level and incorporate, for the six levels, six scores for the 37 characteristics already used. The aim of using the 37 characteristics instead of those from the previous experiment is to report the impact of this category independently of the "vocabulary content" category. Lower perplexity means that the document is more likely to belong to the class in question;
3. Use the new list of characteristics to generate prediction models.

The perplexity score of a document ***D*** is calculated using the formula :

$$PP(D) = \sqrt[n]{\frac{1}{P(m_1 \cdots m_n)}} \qquad (6.1)$$

or :

- $PP(D)$ is the perplexity score of document D;
- $m_1, ..., m_n$ are the words in the text;
- $P(m_1 \cdots m_n)$ is the probability that the sequence of words $m_1, ..., m_n$ occurs in a text.

The equation can also be written, using conditional probability, in the form :

$$PP(D) = \sqrt[n]{\prod_{i=1}^{n} \frac{1}{P(m_i|m_1 \cdots m_{i-1})}} \qquad (6.2)$$

or $P(m_i|m_1 \cdots m_{i-1})$) is the probability that the word m_i is found in a text knowing that the sequence of words m_1 -- - m_{i-1} is found in the text. For bi-gram models, the equation becomes :

$$PP(D) = \sqrt[n]{\prod_{i=1}^{n} \frac{1}{P(m_i|m_{i-1})}} \qquad (6.3)$$

or P (mi-1) is the probability that the word m_i is found in a text knowing that the word that precedes it is found in the same text and is calculated as follows:

$$P(m_i|m_{i-1}) = \frac{\text{nombre d'occurrences du couple } (m_i, m_{i-1})}{\text{nombre d'occurrences de } m_{i-1}} \quad (6.4)$$

number of occurrences of the pair (m_i, mi-1)
number of occurrences of m,-1

Figure 6.7 shows the results of incorporating the perplexity scores in terms of maximum accuracies. We compare the best values obtained using the RF algorithm with those obtained using the initial set of 37 characteristics. For the three classes, we obtained a maximum accuracy of 66.66%, which far exceeds that of the previous experiment (incorporating vocabulary mastery). For the six levels, we obtained a maximum accuracy of 50.0%, which is lower than those obtained in previous experiments.

For the F-measurement, we obtained a value of 0.5 for six levels and 0.69 for three levels (see Figure 6.8).

It should be noted that the results reported are based on LMs compiled from a small corpus, so the impact of this family of characteristics can be improved by increasing the size of the corpus.

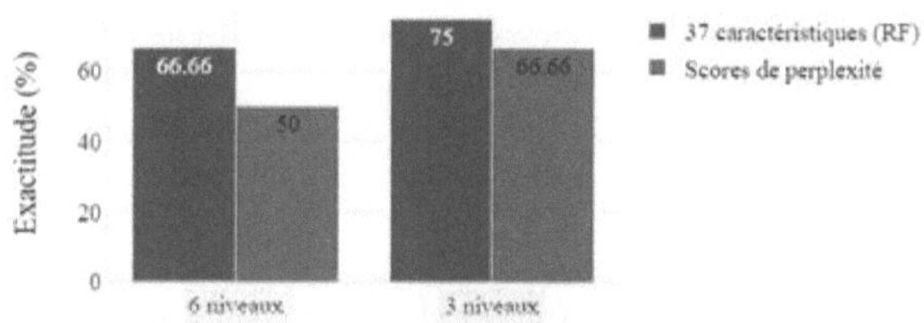

FIG. 6.7 : Maximum accuracy obtained using the perplexity scores

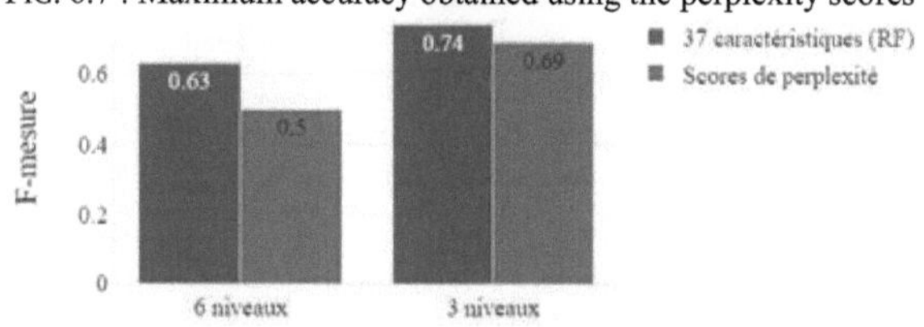

FIG. 6.8 : Maximum F-measures obtained using the perplexity scores

6.6 MoSAR data rebalancing

In this section, we report the results of an experiment carried out using the list of the 37 best L1 features on a balanced training set of the MoSAR corpus.

The process of this experiment, identical to that of L2, consists of :

1. Generate a file containing the vectors representing all the texts in the MoSAR corpus;
2. Perform an initial classification using an 80/20% distribution of the vectors generated using the Random Forest algorithm;
3. Apply the SMOTE technique to the 80% of MoSAR training vectors to balance them. Class "4" is the majority class with a total of 127 vectors. After SMOTE, all classes have the same total (127 vectors).

Table 6.5 shows the accuracy results by level obtained before and after the application of SMOTE.

Comparing the results in Table 6.5, we can conclude that the use of re-equilibration techniques improved the classification results for the independent classes, while maintaining the same maximum value of 67.21%.

	Before SMOTE	After SMOTE
1	0%	25%
2	84,21%	84,21%
3	55,55%	66,66%
4	77,77%	55,55%
5	25%	37,5%
6	91,66%	83,33%
Total	**67,21%**	**67,21%**

Table 6.5: Results of tests on data before and after oversampling

6.7 Conclusion

In this chapter, we have presented the results of the implementation of a set of features in the process of generating predictive models of the readability of Moroccan school texts intended for L1 learners. We have studied the effectiveness of combining classical features with others that are more sophisticated and more closely related to the language under study.

Our process mainly consists of using the MoSAR corpus as a reference corpus, extracting and adapting the set of predictors from L2 to L1, generating models and finally predicting the difficulty of new texts.

Using the six levels of MoSAR, we obtained a maximum accuracy of 68.33% using the initial vector of 37 characteristics to which we incorporated the category of vocabulary mastery based on lemma lexicons. This value was obtained using the SMO algorithm. Finally, we obtained a maximum accuracy of 75% with three classes. This was obtained using the RF algorithm in combination with the vector of the 37 best characteristics.

The number of features adopted in L1 is lower than that adopted in L2. This is due to the fact that the MoSAR corpus is an educational corpus aimed at learners of L1 in primary school, so we can say that the texts in the corpus are easily readable compared with those in L2. If we feed the MoSAR corpus with texts from higher levels, it is likely that we will need more characteristics in order to correctly predict their difficulty levels.

Chapter 7

Simplification of texts

7.1 Introduction

Text Simplification (**TS**) involves reducing the complexity of the vocabulary and sentence structure of a text while preserving its original meaning, with the aim of improving readability. It varies according to the target population: the desired level of text simplification for people with cognitive disabilities (dyslexia [Rello et al., 2013a], autism [Evans et al., 2014], reading difficulties [Gala et al., 2020]) can be very different from that for people without disabilities.

Research in this area has mainly focused on the simplification of English, where corpora with source texts and their associated simplified texts exist and can be automatically aligned, such as the English Wikipedia and the simple English Wikipedia[XVIII] or the Newsela corpus [Xu et al., 2015]. However, data for other languages is difficult to find.

In this chapter, we will review some work on text simplification. Then, we will present the process of an approach for a first attempt in the field of Arabic text simplification.

7.2 General context and related work

The phenomenon of simplification has been going on since the 90s and has continued to develop and become automated over the years. While there has been a lot of work in manual ST over the years, particularly for second language learners, there is less work in automated simplification. The first effort at automated simplification was a grammar and style checker developed for Simplified English editors [Hoard et al., 1992]. Subsequent work has applied phrase-based statistical machine translation techniques to produce simple English [Wubben et al., 2012].

In [Martin et al., 2020], the authors proposed the use of unsupervised extraction techniques to automatically create training corpora for simplification in several languages from raw website data. They evaluated their approach on the basis of simplification criteria in English, French and Spanish.

With the increasing need to produce personalised health information that is readable and comprehensible to the patient, in [Kauchak and Leroy, 2020], the authors presented a text simplification tool that helps medical content producers produce accessible text. The tool uses features that provide concrete suggestions. Tested on a medical corpus, the tool offers good coverage with suggestions on more than a third of words and more than a third of sentences. These suggestions are more than 40% accurate, although the accuracy varies depending on the source of the text. They have adopted both word-level and sentence-level approaches.

We can group all the techniques presented in this field into four families, namely :

The lexical approach: for a given text, this involves identifying and replacing complex words with simpler substitutions. It involves three stages:

1. Identifying complex words ;
2. For each complex word, a list of substitutions is generated, ranked in order of simplicity;
3. Use the simplest synonym to replace the original word.

In addition to single-word substitution, lexical substitution can also be carried out at sentence level. This requires a command of the target language. A sentence can be replaced by a single word that expresses the same thing or by another sentence that uses simpler language.

The syntactic approach: consists of identifying the grammatical complexities of a text and rewriting them in simpler structures. This technique can be applied to many types of syntactic

XVIII `https://simple.wikipedia.org/wiki/Main_Page` (last visited 08/11/2020)

complexity:

- Long sentences can be divided into several phrases;
- Sentences in the passive voice can be rewritten in the active voice.

The explanation generation approach: consists of taking a difficult concept in a text and enriching it with additional information, which puts it into context and improves the user's understanding.

The statistical machine translation approach: consists of studying ST as a case of complex-to-simple text generation. The translation task is then considered as a conversion from the complex source language X to the same target language X, but simpler. Each of these languages has its own syntax and lexicon to allow the use of auto-matic translation techniques.

Research in the field of machine translation is mainly based on statistical and neural methods [Junczys-Dowmunt et al., 2016]. Statistical methods require bilingual corpora aligned at sentence level. Neural methods require large parallel corpora. To our knowledge, these types of corpora are not available for Arabic.

Concerning the Arabic language, [Al Khalil et al., 2017] described in their work the motivation and outline of a project called ***SAMER*** (Simplification of Arabic Masterpieces for Extensive Reading), which focuses on the simplification of a collection of novels. The project involves rewriting the collection of novels in a simple style that can be read by school-age learners. Several researchers in Arabic literature and pedagogy contributed to the project. The task of simplification was carried out by experts, who followed a set of general guidelines to achieve changes in vocabulary, structure, style and detail.

7.3 Proposal for a lexical simplification approach for the Arabic language

In this section, we present a lexical simplification process which exploits the various resources developed in the course of this research. For a given text, the process consists of :

1. Detect the level of difficulty using the best models for predicting readability in L1 and L2 that we developed in Chapters 5 and 6 ;
2. Simplify the lexicon of complex words ;
3. Check whether the new text is less complex than the original.

7.3.1 Lexical simplification of complex words

During this phase, the system must be able to scan the text and identify complex words and simplify them. To do this, it is necessary to extract the words from the text, then search for them in a list of synonyms in order to replace them with their simpler synonyms. The process used for this step is as follows:

1. Use the PoS-tagging results to identify which words do not need to be simplified and which do. It is clear that some words, such as proper nouns (Alam) and prepositions (Pr and PCo), do not need to be simplified. Table 7.1 shows the list of tags that we have excluded from the simplification phase;

PoS	Description	Description arabe	Exemple
Pronom	Pronom	ضمير منفصل	هُوَ/huwa
Alam	Nom propre	اسم علم	مُحَمَّد/muHamãd
NoDP	Pronom démonstratif	اسم إشارة	ذَلِكَ/*alika
NoRP	Pronom relatif	اسم موصول	الَّتِي/Alãtiy
PCo	Préposition + Pronom	جار ومجرور	لَهُ/lahu
Pr	Préposition	حَرْف جَر	عَنْ/Eano
Co	Conjonction de coordination	حرف عطف	أَوْ/>awo
PaNs	Particule du subjonctif	حرف ناصِب	أَنْ/>ano
La	Particule de négation ou d'interdiction	لا الناهية أو النافية	لَا/LaA
CJ	Particules de l'apocopé	حرف جزم	لَمْ/lamo
Abrv	Abréviation	مختصر	إلخ/<lx
PNa	Inna et ses analogues	حرف ناسِخ	أَنَّ>anã
Ex	Particule d'exception	أداة استثناء	إِلَّا/<lAã
Interj	interjections vocatives	حرف نداء	يَا/yaA

Table 7.1: List of PoS tags excluded from the simplification phase

2. Based on the assumption that, if a word is part of the lexicon of the desired level, it should not be simplified, we will keep all the words in the desired lexicon;
3. The remaining words will be the subject of a synonym search. To do this, we used the **AWN** (Arabic WordNet) API [Black et al., 2006], to retrieve a list of all possible synonyms for a given word using the AWN database. The list is ordered by simplicity. A word is simple if it is found in the frequency dictionary;
4. Replace a complex word with its simplest synonym. Note that words which have no synonyms (the list of synonyms re-turned by AWN is empty), those whose synonym is the word itself and those for which no synonym is simple will be kept;
5. Finally, detect the level of difficulty of the new text.

7.3.2 Experiments and results

In this section, we will apply the approach we presented in section 7.3.1 to the MoSAR corpus for L1 and the GLOSS-Reading corpus for L2. We will use the distribution of these corpora into three classes: easy, medium and difficult. For this experiment, we will try to simplify the texts which belong to the difficult class.

Applying the first three steps of the process (see section 7.3.1) has enabled us to reduce the set of texts on which we will apply the tests. Table 7.2 shows the size of the test sets before and after the application of these steps in the process. Ignored texts are texts for which all the complex words do not have frequent synonyms in the "AWN" database.

Corpus	All difficult texts	Number of test texts
GLOSS-Reading	114	113
MoSAR	216	163

Table 7.2: Size of simplification corpus

For MoSAR, 53 texts were ignored, whereas for GLOSS-Reading only one text had no synonyms and so we kept 113 texts from this corpus for the rest of the process.

The *AWN* database, from which we drew synonyms, contains 11,269 sets of synonyms which are classified according to four PoS tags (verb, noun, adjective and adverb). Table 7.3 shows the statistics for this database.

AWN contains 7,960 nouns and only 2,538 verbs, which explains the absence of synonyms from previously ignored texts.

Applying the fourth stage of the process to the remaining texts, a number of complex words were replaced by simpler and more frequent equivalents. Table 7.4 lists some examples of these words.

PoS	Size
Name	7 960
Verb	2 538
Adjective	661
Adverb	110
Total	**11 269**

Table 7.3: Distribution of the AWN database by grammatical category

Complex words	Simple equivalent	Translation
Mots complexe	**Équivalent simple**	**Traduction**
رمز / rmz	علامة / ElAmp	Signe
تكرار / tkrAr	إعادة / <EAdp	Répétition
فجوة / fjwp	فتحة / ftHp	Écart
وكر / wkr	عش / E$	Nid
منوال / mnwAl	طريقة / Tryqp	Méthode
توليد / twlyd	إنتاج / <ntAj	Production

Table 7.4: Examples of simplified words

For this replacement step, for example, we have the sentence "المشروع مخصص فقط لتوليد الكهرباء وليس لاستهلاك المياه (The project is intended solely for the production of electricity and not for the consumption of water)" which contains the complex word "توليد" which, out of context, means "generation". This word has been replaced by the simple word "إنتاج" which means "production" and so the first sentence is replaced by the sentence "المشروع مخصص فقط لإنتاج الكهرباء وليس لاستهلاك المياه" which is still translated as "The project is intended solely for the production of electricity and not for the consumption of water".

After replacing the complex words with their simple equivalents, we recalculated the difficulty level of the new texts and compared the results with the original difficulty levels of the texts. Table 7.5 shows the number of simplified texts for each corpus.

Corpus	Number of simplified texts
MoSAR	28
GLOSS-Reading	19

Table 7.5: Number of simplified texts

For the MoSAR corpus, 28 texts were simplified while the remaining 135 texts could not be simplified. Among these 135 texts, we have :

- 47 texts containing a single word with a simple synonym ;
- 37 texts that have two words with a simple synonym.

For these two sets, the modified text does not have a large change compared to the original text, which does not allow the level of the text to be changed. For the 28 simplified texts, the number of complex words replaced varied from 3 to 8 words.

For the GLOSS-Reading corpus, 19 texts were simplified. Among the 94 remaining texts, we have :

- A single text that has a single word with a simple synonym;
- Ten texts that have two words with a simple synonym;
- Five texts that have three words with a simple synonym.

Unlike MoSAR, the number of complex words replaced in simplified texts varies from 4 to 15 words.

In a second experiment, we performed the simplification process on a set of 100 texts taken from the "HindaouiCorpus". All 100 texts were classified ***using*** the L1 readability prediction models. Table 7.6 presents the results of this second experiment.

	Easy	Medium	Difficult
100 difficult texts	2	72	26

Table 7.6: Simplification results on HindaouiCorpus

HindaouiCorpus showed better simplification results than the two previous corpora, with 74 simplified texts.

From these results, we can conclude that lexical simplification plays an important role in changing the difficulty levels of texts. To improve the results of this first approach, we can envisage transformations at the level of :

1. **Words:** replacing a word by a set of words (for example, replacing the word سيدخلون] by (سوف يدخلون) ;

2. **Sentences:** for example, change the passive voice to the active voice, break up long sentences into shorter ones, etc.

7.4 Conclusion

In this chapter, we have reviewed some text simplification approaches for foreign languages and for Arabic, and we have highlighted the challenges facing this field of NLP research.

We have proposed a prototype for simplifying Arabic texts. Such a system would greatly contribute to generating readable and accessible content for low-literacy users, children and Arabic learners. The proposed approach describes a set of main steps that would lead to the simplification of Arabic corpora along with the set of technologies and tools that would facilitate the implementation of these steps. Throughout these steps, difficulties, gaps and obstacles are identified and proposed as research themes and perspectives for this work in order to improve research related to the simplification and readability of the Arabic language.

We have tested this approach on three different corpora (MoSAR, GLOSS-Reading and HindaouiCorpus), two of which are annotated in difficulty levels by specialists, and the third is a corpus that we used in the development of the frequency dictionary. The results of this first attempt are encouraging.

Chapter 8

Conclusion and outlook

The main objective of this research was to improve the results presented by many researchers in order to design and implement models for the self-prediction of the difficulty level of the Arabic language. In this thesis, we are interested in predicting the readability of educational texts intended for learners of Arabic as a first language (L1) and as a second or foreign language (L2). To develop these models, we adopted a three-stage approach: (1) a morphological analysis stage, (2) a feature extraction stage, and (3) finally a learning and prediction model generation stage.

Entering the morphological annotation phase requires a corpus annotated by difficulty level. Given the unavailability of such resources, we developed and collected four educational corpora annotated by readability levels according to well-defined scales. The first corpus is dedicated to learners of Arabic as L1 and was collected from books in the Moroccan school system. This corpus, which we have named MoSAR (Modern Standard Arabic Readability), is composed of 602 texts and 77,966 words divided into six difficulty levels. The three remaining corpora are dedicated to L2 learners. These are collected from two different resources:

1. The GLOSS platform from which we have collected two corpora:
   - GLOSS-Reading is a corpus made up of 271 reading texts and 95,496 words;
   - GLOSS-Learning is a corpus made up of 227 listening texts and 56,684 words.
2. The Aljazeera-Learning website, from which we have collected a corpus consisting of 321 texts and 49,345 words.

These three corpora are annotated according to five levels of difficulty based on the ILR scale, an international scale for annotating texts intended for independent learners of foreign languages. As mentioned above, the corpora are used as input for the morphological annotation phase, which was carried out using the two morphological analysers MADAMIRA and Alkhalil-Toolkit.

The second phase of the approach adopted consists in extracting a list of characteristics that we have well-defined from the morphological information obtained in the first step. Most of these characteristics are calculated using a frequency dictionary we have developed, which provides a list of the 5,000 most frequent lemmas and their morphological and statistical information.

Finally, we developed a set of models for predicting L1 and L2 readability. We also adapted the list of features for each language type (L1 or L2). Our models performed well. We obtained a maximum accuracy of 81.81%, 82.22%, 87.69%, and 75% for GLOSS-Reading, GLOSS-Listening, Aljazeera-Learning and MoSAR respectively and we obtained a maximum F-measure value of 0.82 for the three L2 corpora and a maximum F-measure value of 0.74 for L1 with the MoSAR corpus.

We have also presented in the manuscript of this thesis a proposed approach to the simplification of L1 and L2 texts. The results of the first tests of this study are encouraging.

Outlook

From the results of all the tests we have presented in this thesis, which are very encouraging, we can conclude that these methods suffer from several weaknesses that we will seek to overcome in our future work, such as :

- The lack of annotated resources for developing and evaluating mo- deles. Hence the first area of work for the future is to improve the MoSAR corpus by adding new texts and covering new school levels. A second avenue is to build corpora for learners with specific needs (people with learning disabilities, the visually impaired, etc.);
- The choice of features to be extracted varies from one corpus to another. As a result, we also

need to study the use of advanced learning methods, which automate the choice and extraction of features (they are not fixed in advance), but require large corpora.

- Readability tools need to be extended to include syntax and semantics, but this requires the availability of tools and resources to support it.
- Finally, more fundamental research is needed in the area of text simplification. We can improve this work by a more in-depth investigation into syntactic simplification, which consists of decomposing and modifying the syntax of long and complex sentences. The use of machine translation is a possible direction for ST.

Appendix A
Examples of texts in the frequency dictionary

Table A.1 shows the annotation of the sentence "أشهد أن لا إله إلا الله وحده لا شريك له وأشهد أن سيدنا محمدا عبده ورسوله" extracted from the Tashkeela+ corpus, using Alkhalil-Toolkit. Table A.2 shows the same annotated sentence using MADAMIRA.

Tag in Arabic	PoS	Translitteration	Lemma	Word
Tag en arabe	**PoS**	**Translittération**	**Lemme**	**Mot**
فعل مضارع	VeP	$ahida	شَهِدَ	أشهد
حرف ناصِب	PaNs	>an~a	أَنَّ	أن
لا الناهية أو النافية	La	laA	لَا	لا
اسم	No	<ilah	إِلَه	إله
أداة استثناء	Ex	<lA	إِلا	إلا
اسم علم	Alam	All~ah	الله	الله
اسم + مضاف إليه	No.S	waHod	وَحْد	وحده
لا الناهية أو النافية	La	laA	لَا	لا
صفة	Sifa	$ariyk	شَرِيك	شريك
جار ومجرور	PCo	waliya	وَلِيَ	له
حرف عطف + فعل مضارع	Conj P.VeP	$ahida	شَهِدَ	وأشهد
حرف ناسِخ	PNa	>an~a	أَنَّ	أن
اسم + مضاف إليه	No.S	say~id	سَيِّد	سيدنا
صفة	Sifa	muHam~ad	مُحَمَّد	محمدا
اسم + مضاف إليه	No.S	Eabod	عَبْد	عبده
حرف عطف + صفة + مضاف إليه	Conj P.Sifa.S	rasuwl	رَسُول	ورسوله

Table A.1: Extract from a Tashkeela+ text annotated by Alkhalil-Toolkit

The two tables show differences in lemmas and PoS. These differences can be grouped into two families:

1. Differences in the tags used by the two analysers, but which represent the majority of the tags used.

Tag in Arabic	PoS	Translitteration	Lemma	Word
Tag en arabe	PoS	Translittération	Lemme	Mot
فعل	verb	$ahid	شَهِد	أشهد
أداة ربط	conj_sub	>an~a	أَنَّ	أن
شبه فعل	verb_pseudo	lA	لا	لا
اسم	noun	waliy	وَلِي	إله
أداة استثناء	part_restrict	<il~A	إِلّا	إلا
اسم علم	noun_prop	All~ah	الله	الله
اسم	noun	Had~	حَدّ	وحده
شبه فعل	verb_pseudo	lA	لا	لا
اسم	noun	$ariyk	شَرِيك	شريك
حرف جر	prep	li	لِ	له
فعل	verb	$ahid	شَهِد	وأشهد
شبه فعل	verb_pseudo	>an~a	أَنَّ	أن
اسم	noun	>adAn	أدان	سيدنا
اسم علم	noun_prop	mHmdA	محمدا	محمدا
اسم علم	noun_prop	Eabod	عَبْد	عبده
اسم	noun	rasuwl	رَسُول	ورسوله

Table A.2: Extract from a Tashkeela+ text annotated by MADAMIRA

same grammatical category: for example, both parsers assign the verb label to the word "أشهد", except that Alkhalil-Toolkit gives more details. In the first appearance it specifies the verb tense (VeP = verb in the present tense) and in the second appearance it specifies, in addition to the verb tense, that the word contains a conjunction-type prefix which is the letter 'وْ' . For the word " الله" , which is a proper noun, MADAMIRA assigns it the tag "noun_prop", whereas Alkhalil-Toolkit assigns it the tag "Alam";

2. Differences due to annotation errors by one of the two analysers: for example, the word "محمدا" is annotated as an adjective using Alkhalil-Toolkit whereas MADAMIRA annotates it correctly as a proper noun. For the word "سيدنا", MADAMIRA assigns it the incorrect lemma "أدان" whereas Alkhalil-Toolkit correctly lemmatises it as "سَيِّد".

Appendix B
Extracts from the MoSAR corpus

B.1 Extract in JSON format


```
{''book'' : {
    ''id'' : 1,
    ''level'' : 1,
    ''text'' : {
                    ...
        ''segment_info'' : {
            ''id'' : 4,
            ''sentence'' : ''تُفِيقُ سَلْمَى مُبَكِّرًا كُلَّ صَبَاحٍ.'',
            ''analysis'' : {
                ''nb'' : 5,
                ''morph_feature_set'' : [
                    {
                        ''id'' : 1,
                        ''word'' : ''تُفِيقُ'',
                        ''stem'' : ''تُفِيقُ'',
                        ''lemma'' : ''أَفَاقَ'',
                        ''root'' : ''فيق'',
                        ''pos'' : ''VeP''
                    },

                    {
                        ''id'' : 2,
                        ''word'' : ''سَلْمَى'',

                        ''stem'' : ''سَلْمَى'',
                        ''lemma'' : ''سَلْمَى'',
                        ''root'' : ''–'',
                        ''pos'' : ''Alam''
                    },    ...
                ]
            } },

        ''id'' : 1,
        ''week'' : 1,
        ''type'' : ''Expression'',
        ''title'' : ''فِي الصَّبَاحِ''
    },
    ''title'' : ''كتابي في اللغة العربية''
}}
```

B.2 Extract in text format

```
book :
    title : كتابي في اللغة العربية
    level :1
    id :1
text :
    week :1
    id :1
    type :Expression
    title : فِي الصَّبَاحِ
...
segment_info :
    sentence :".تُفِيقُ سَلْمَى مُبَكِّرًا كُلَّ صَبَاحٍ"
    id :4
words :
    id :1    word :تُفِيقُ    stem :تُفِيقُ    lemma :فَاقَ    root :فيق    pos :VeP
    id :2    word :سَلْمَى    stem :سَلْمَى    lemma :سَلْمَى    root :–    pos :Alam
    id :3    word :مُبَكِّرًا    stem :مُبَكِّرًا    lemma :مُبَكِّر    root :بكر    pos :Sifa
...
```

Appendix C
Complete list of features

Table C.1: List of 170 characteristics

Category	Features	Description
Average **sentence** length	SL1	The number of sentences in a text
	SL2	Average sentence length in words = number of words / number of sentences
	SL3	Average sentence length in characters = number of characters / number of sentences
	SL4	Average sentence length in stems = number of stems / number of sentences
Average word length **(Word Length)**	WL1	The number of words in a text
	WL2	Average stem word length = number of stems / number of words
	WL3	Average word length in characters = number of characters / number of words
	WL4	The number of stems in a text
	WL5	The number of characters in a text
Word Class	WC1	The number of open-class words in a text (e.g. noun, verb, etc.)
	WC2	The ratio of open class words to total words in a text
	WC3	The number of closed words in a text (e.g. conjunctions, prepositions, etc.)

Continued on next page

Tab. C.1 - continued from previous page

Category	Features	Description
	WC4	The ratio between closed class words and the total number of words in a text
Ambiguite **(Ambiguite)**	AMb1	The number of ambiguous lemmas (lemmas that obtain several distinct PoS tags)
	AMb2	The ratio of ambiguous lemmas to total words in a text
	AMb3	The ratio of ambiguous lemmas to total lemmas in a text
Vocabulary load	VL1	The number of distinct lemmas in a text
	VL2	The number of frequent lemmas (lemmas appearing more than once) in a text
	VL3	The ratio of frequent lemmas to total words in a text
Word to word ratio **(Type-To-W Token**	TTR1	The ratio of lemmas to total words
	TTR2	The ratio of stems to total words
	TTR3	The square root of TTR2
	TTR4	The square root of TTR1
Foreign	FW1	The ratio of foreign words to total words
Word and lemma sequences	TTF1	The ratio of frequent lemmas to total words
	TTF2	Maximum dispersion of frequent lemmas
	TTF3	The maximum rank of frequent lemmas

Category	Features	Description
	TTF4	The average dispersion of frequent words
	TTF5	The average dispersion of frequent lemmas
	TTF6	The average rank of frequent lemmas

Continued on next page

Tab. C.1 - continued from previous page

Category	Features	Description
(Token and Type Frequency)	TTF7	The average rank of frequent words
	TTF8	Median dispersion of frequent words
	TTF9	The median dispersion of frequent lemmas
	TTF10	The median rank of frequent lemmas
	TTF11	The median rank of frequent words
	TTF12	The minimum dispersion of frequent lemmas
	TTF13	The minimum rank of frequent lemmas
	TTF14	The range of frequent lemmas
	TTF15	The range of dispersions of frequent lemmas
	TTF16	The ratio of frequent words to total stems
	TTF17	The ratio of frequent lemmas to total stems
Ratios between lemma PoS and words **(Type To Token POS Ratio)**	TTPR1	The ratio of adjectives to total words
	TTPR2	The ratio of comparative adjectives to total words
	TTPR3	The ratio of numeric adjectives to total words
	TTPR4	The ratio of adverbs to total words
	TTPR5	The ratio of relational adverbs to total words
	TTPR6	The ratio of conjunctions to total words
	TTPR7	The ratio of subordinating conjunctions to total words
	TTPR8	The ratio of names to total words
	TTPR9	The ratio of numerical names to total words
	TTPR10	The ratio of proper nouns to total words
	TTPR11	The ratio of quantitative nouns to total words
	TTPR12	The ratio of particles to total words
	TTPR13	The ratio of focal particles to total words
	TTPR14	The ratio of interrogative particles to total words
	TTPR15	The ratio of negative particles to total words

Continued on next page

Tab. C.1 - continued from previous page

Category	Features	Description
	TTPR16	The ratio of verbal particles to total words
	TTPR17	The ratio of prepositions to total words
	TTPR18	The ratio of pronouns to total words
	TTPR19	The ratio of demonstrative pronouns to total words
	TTPR20	The ratio of relative pronouns to total words
	TTPR21	The ratio of punctuation to total words
	TTPR22	The ratio of verbs to total words
	TTPR23	The ratio of pseudo-verbs to total words
	TTPR24	The ratio between adjectives and open class words
	TTPR25	The ratio between adverbs and open class words
	TTPR26	The ratio between verbs and open class words

	TTPR27	The number of nouns in a text
	TTPR28	The number of adverbs in a text
	TTPR29	The number of proper nouns in a text
	TTPR30	The number of adjectives and comparative adjectives in a text
	TTPR31	The number of verbs in a text
	TTPR32	The ratio between nouns and open class words
	TTPR33	The ratio between proper nouns and open class words
	PBF1	The ratio of frequent adjectives to total adjectives
	PBF2	The ratio between frequent lemmas whose PoS tag begins with adjective and the total number of lemmas whose PoS tag begins with adjective (adj*)
	PBF3	The ratio of frequent subordinating conjunctions to total subordinating conjunctions
	PBF4	The ratio of frequent conjunctions to total conjunctions
	PBF5	The ratio between frequent lemmas whose PoS tag begins with conjunction and the total number of lemmas whose PoS tag begins with conjunction (conj*)
Continued on next page		

Tab. C.1 - continued from previous page

Category	Features	Description
PoS-based frequencies (**POS Based Frequency**)	PBF6	The ratio of frequent numeric names to total numeric names
	PBF7	The ratio of frequent proper names to total proper names
	PBF8	The ratio of frequent quantitative nouns to total quantitative nouns
	PBF9	The ratio of frequent names to total names
	PBF10	The ratio of frequent lemmas whose PoS tag begins with name to the total number of lemmas whose PoS tag begins with name (noun*)
	PBF11	The ratio between frequent lemmas whose PoS tag begins with particle and the total number of lemmas whose PoS tag begins with particle (part*)
	PBF12	The ratio of frequent prepositions to total prepositions
	PBF13	The ratio of frequent demonstrative pronouns to total demonstrative pronouns
	PBF14	The ratio of frequent relative pronouns to total relative pronouns
	PBF15	The ratio between frequent lemmas whose PoS tag begins with pronoun and the total number of lemmas whose PoS tag begins with pronoun (pron*)
	PBF16	The ratio of frequent verbs to total verbs
	PBF17	The maximum rank of frequent adjectives
	PBF18	The maximum rank of frequent lemmas whose PoS tag begins with adjective (adj*)
	PBF19	The maximum rank of frequent lemmas whose PoS tag begins with conjunction (conj*)

	PBF20	The maximum rank of frequent lemmas whose PoS tag begins with name (noun*)
	PBF21	The maximum rank of frequent lemmas whose PoS tag begins with particle (part*)
	PBF22	The maximum rank of frequent lemmas whose PoS tag begins with pronoun (pron*)

Continued on next page

Tab. C.1 - continued from previous page

Category	Features	Description
	PBF23	The maximum rank of free subordinating conjunctions
	PBF24	The maximum rank of frequent conjunctions
	PBF25	The maximum rank of frequent numeric names
	PBF26	Maximum rank for frequent proper nouns
	PBF27	The maximum rank of frequent quantitative nouns
	PBF28	The maximum rank of frequent names
	PBF29	The maximum rank of frequent prepositions
	PBF30	The maximum rank of frequent demonstrative pronouns
	PBF31	The maximum rank of frequent relative pronouns
	PBF32	The maximum rank of frequent verbs
	PBF33	The average rank of frequent adjectives
	PBF34	The average rank of frequent lemmas whose PoS tag begins with adjective (adj*)
	PBF35	The average rank of frequent lemmas whose PoS tag begins with conjunction (conj*)
	PBF36	The average rank of frequent lemmas whose PoS tag begins with name (noun*)
	PBF37	The average rank of frequent lemmas whose PoS tag begins with particle (part*)
	PBF38	The average rank of frequent lemmas whose PoS tag begins with pronoun (pron*)
	PBF39	The average rank of free subordinating conjunctions
	PBF40	The average rank of frequent conjunctions
	PBF41	The average rank of frequent numeric names
	PBF42	The average rank of frequent proper names
	PBF43	The average rank of frequent quantitative nouns
	PBF44	The average rank of frequent names
	PBF45	The average rank of frequent prepositions
	PBF46	The average rank of frequent demonstrative pronouns
	PBF47	The average rank of frequent relative pronouns
	PBF48	The average rank of frequent verbs
	PBF49	The median rank of frequent adjectives

Continued on next page

Tab. C.1 - continued from previous page

Category	Features	Description
	PBF50	The median rank of frequent lemmas whose PoS tag begins with adjective (adj*)

	PBF51	The median rank of frequent lemmas whose PoS tag begins with conjunction (conj*)
	PBF52	The median rank of frequent lemmas whose PoS tag begins with name (noun*)
	PBF53	The median rank of frequent lemmas whose PoS tag begins with particle (part*)
	PBF54	The median rank of frequent lemmas whose PoS tag begins with pronoun (pron*)
	PBF55	The median rank of free subordinating conjunctions
	PBF56	The median rank of frequent conjunctions
	PBF57	The median rank of frequent numeric names
	PBF58	The median rank of common proper names
	PBF59	The median rank of frequent quantitative nouns
	PBF60	The median rank of frequent names
	PBF61	The median rank of frequent prepositions
	PBF62	The median rank of frequent demonstrative pronouns
	PBF63	The median rank of frequent relative pronouns
	PBF64	The median rank of frequent verbs
	PBF65	The minimum rank of frequent adjectives
	PBF66	The minimum rank of frequent lemmas whose PoS tag begins with adjective (adj*)
	PBF67	The minimum rank of frequent lemmas whose PoS tag begins with conjunction (conj*)
	PBF68	The minimum rank of frequent lemmas whose PoS tag begins with name (noun*)
	PBF69	The minimum rank of frequent lemmas whose PoS tag begins with particle (part*)
	PBF70	The minimum rank of frequent lemmas whose PoS tag begins with pronoun (pron*)
	PBF71	The minimum rank of free subordinating conjunctions

Continued on next page

Tab. C.1 - continued from previous page

Category	Features	Description
	PBF72	The minimum rank of frequent conjunctions
	PBF73	The minimum rank of frequent numeric names
	PBF74	The minimum rank of frequent proper names
	PBF75	The minimum rank of frequent quantitative nouns
	PBF76	The minimum rank of frequent names
	PBF77	The minimum rank of frequent prepositions
	PBF78	The minimum rank of frequent demonstrative pronouns
	PBF79	The minimum rank of frequent relative pronouns
	PBF80	The minimum rank of frequent verbs
	PBF81	The range of ranks for frequent adjectives
	PBF82	The range of frequent lemmas whose PoS tag begins with adjective (adj*)
	PBF83	The range of ranks for frequent lemmas whose PoS tag

		begins with conjunction (conj*)
	PBF84	The range of ranks of frequent lemmas whose PoS tag begins with name (noun*)
	PBF85	The range of ranks for frequent lemmas whose PoS tag begins with particle (part*)
	PBF86	The range of frequent lemmas whose PoS tag begins with pronoun (pron*)
	PBF87	The range of ranks of free subordinating conjunctions
	PBF88	The range of ranks for frequent conjunctions
	PBF89	The range of frequent numeric names
	PBF90	The range of frequent proper names
	PBF91	The range of ranks for frequent quantitative nouns
	PBF92	The range of frequent noun ranks
	PBF93	The range of ranks for frequent prepositions
	PBF94	The range of ranks of frequent demonstrative pronouns
	PBF95	The range of frequent relative pronouns
	PBF96	The range of frequent verb ranks

Appendix D
Pseudo-code for the algorithm SMOTE

SMOTE(T, N, k) **algorithm**

Input: Number of samples in minority class T; SMOTE rate N%; Number of nearest neighbours k

Output: (N/100) * T synthetical samples of the minority class

/* If N is less than 100%, select samples from the minority class at random, as only a random percentage of them will be analysed (SMOTEd). */**If** N < 100

then randomly distribute the samples from the minority class T

T = (N/100) * T

N= 100

FinSi

N = (int)(N/100) /* The SMOTE rate is assumed to be an integer multiple of 100. */

k = Number of nearest neighbours

numattrs = Number of attributes

Sample[ ][ ] : table for original samples of the minority class

newindex: keeps track of the number of synthetic samples generated, initialized at a0

Synthetic[ ][ ] : table for synthetic samples

/* Calculate k nearest neighbours for each sample in the minority class. */

for i ← 1 **a** T

Compute k nearest neighbors for i, and save the indices in the nnarray

Populate(N, i, nnarray)

FinFor

Populate(N, i, nnarray) /* Function for generating synthetic samples. */

while N 0 #

Choose a random number between 1 and k, call it nn. This step allows us to choose one of i's k nearest neighbours.

for attr ← **1 a** numattrs

Calculate: dif = Sample[nnarray[nn]][attr] - Sample[i][attr]

Calculate: gap = random number between 0 and 1

Synthetic[newindex][attr] = Sample[i][attr] + gap * dif

FinFor

newindex++

N=N-1

FinWhile

return /*End of Populate. */

End of the Pseudo-Code.

Publications

Articles published in indexed journals

1. **N.Nassiri**, A.Lakhouaja , V.Cavalli-Sforza, **Readability Assessment of educational texts in Arabic L2**, International Journal of Knowledge and Learning (under review).
2. **N.Nassiri**, A.Lakhouaja , V.Cavalli-Sforza, **Arabic L2 Readability Assessment: Dimensionality Reduction Study**, Journal of King Saud University - Computer and Information Sciences, **2021**, ISSN 1319-1578.
DOI : 10.1016/j.jksuci.2020.12.021.
3. Cavalli-Sforza, V.; Saddiki, H.; **Nassiri, N.**; **2018**. *Arabic Readability Research: Current State and Future Directions*. Procedia Computer Science. Volume 142, 2018, Pages 38-49. **DOI :** 10.1016/j.procs.2018.10.459.

Papers published in indexed conferences

1. **Nassiri, N.** ; Lakhouaja, A.; Cavalli-Sforza, V.; **2021**. *combining classical and non-classical features to improve readability measures for arabic first language texts*. In: Proceedings of the International Conference on Advanced Intelligent Systems for Sustainable Development (AI2SD), Tangier, Morocco, December 21-26, 2020.
2. **Nassiri, N.**; Cavalli-Sforza, V.; Lakhouaja, A.; **2019**. *MoSAR: Modern Standard Arabic Readability Corpus for L1 Learners*. In: Proceedings of the 4th International Conference On Big Data and Internet of Things (BDIoT), Rabat, Morocco, October 23-24, 2019. **DOI :** 10.1145/3372938.3372961. ACM; SCOPUS; ...
3. **Nassiri, N.**; Lakhouaja, A.; Cavalli-Sforza, V.; **2018**. *Arabic Readability Assessment for Foreign Language Learners*. In: Silberztein M., Atigui F., Kornyshova E., Metais E., Meziane F. (eds) Natural Language Processing and Information Systems. NLDB 2018. Lecture Notes in Computer Science, vol 10859. Springer, Cham. **DOI :** 10.1007/978-3-319-91947-8_49. WEB OF SCIENCE; SCOPUS; ...
4. **Nassiri, N.**; Lakhouaja, A.; Cavalli-Sforza, V.; **2018**. *Modern Standard Arabic Readability Prediction*. In: Lachkar A., Bouzoubaa K., Mazroui A., Hamdani A., Lekhouaja A. (eds) Arabic Language Processing: From Theory to Practice. ICALP 2017. Communications in Computer and Information Science, vol 782. Springer, Cham. **DOI :** 10.1007/978-3-319-73500-9_9. WEB OF SCIENCE; SCOPUS; ...

Papers published at national and international conferences

1. **Nassiri, N.**; Lakhouaja, A.; Cavalli-Sforza, V.; **2019**. *Automatic difficulty evaluation of Arabic texts*. In the Mathematics and Computer Science Doctoral Day, February 2020.Oujda, Morocco.
2. **Nassiri, N.**; Cavalli-Sforza, V.; Lakhouaja, A.; **2019**. *Relevant Features Selection in Readability Assessment*. In the second conference on linguistic diversity and NLP (DiLiTAL) December 2019.Oujda, Morocco.
3. **Nassiri, N.**; Lakhouaja, A.; Cavalli-Sforza, V.; **2019**. *An Arabic L1 Corpus-based Readability Evaluation*. In the International Conference on Advanced Technologies and Humanitarian Sciences. ICATHS July 2019.
4. **Nassiri, N.**; Lakhouaja, A.; Cavalli-Sforza, V.; **2018**. *Construction of an Arabic corpus of school texts*. In 3eme Journee Doctorale sur l'Ingenierie de la Langue Arabe (JDILA'18) Thursday, November 1, 2018.

Bibliography

N. Ababou and A. Mazroui. A hybrid Arabic POS tagging for simple and compound morphosyntactic tags. *International Journal of Speech Technology,* 19(2) :289-302, June 2016. ISSN 1572-8110. doi : 10.1007/s10772-015-9302-8. (Cite on page 45)

A. Abubaker and J. Lu. The optimum font size and type for students aged 9-12 reading Arabic characters on screen: A case study. *Journal of Physics: Conference Series*, 364, 05 2012. doi : 10.1088/1742-6596/364/1/012115 (Cite on page 10)

A. Al-Ajlan, H. Al-Khalifa, and A.-M. Al-Salman. Towards the development of an automatic readability measurements for arabic language. pages 506 - 511, 12 2008. doi : 10.1109/ICDIM.2008.4746711. (Cite on page 19)

S. Al-Aqeel, N. Abanmy, A. Aldayel, H. Al-Khalifa, M. Al-yahya, and M. Diab. Readability of written medicine information materials in Arabic language: Expert and consumer evaluation. *BMC Health Services Research*, 18:139, 02 2018. doi: 10.1186/ s12913-018-2944-x. (Cite on page 35)

M. Al-Batal. Playing with words: Teaching vocabulary in the Arabic curriculum. 2006. (Quoted on page 40)

F. Al-Busaidi, A. Alhashmi, A. Al-Musawi, and A. Kadhim. Teachers' perceptions on the effectiveness of using Arabic language teaching software in omani basic education. *International Journal of Education and Development using Information and Communication Technology*, 12(2) :139-157, 2016. ISSN 1814-0556 (Cite on page 52)

H. Al-Khalifa and A. Al-Ajlan. Automatic readability measurements of the arabic text: An exploratory study. *Arabian Journal for Science and Engineering*, 35:103-124, 12 2010. (Cited on pages xi, 1, 31, 32, 33 and 51)

M. Al Khalil, N. Habash, and H. Saddiki. Simplification of Arabic masterpieces for extensive reading: A project overview. *Procedia Computer Science*, 117:192 - 198, 2017. ISSN 1877-0509. doi: https://doi.org/10.1016/j.procs.2017.10.109. URL http://www.sciencedirect.com/science/article/pii/S187705091732166X. Arabic Computational Linguistics (Cite page 105)

M. Al Khalil, H. Saddiki, N. Habash, and L. Alfalasi. A leveled reading corpus of Modern Standard Arabic. In *Proceedings of the Eleventh International Conference on Language Resources and Evaluation (LREC 2018)*, Miyazaki, Japan, May 2018. European Language Resources Association (ELRA). URL https://www.aclweb.org/anthology/ L18-1366. (Cited on pages 32 and 51)

L. Al-Sulaiti, N. Abbas, C. Brierley, E. Atwell, and A. Alghamdi. Compilation of an Arabic children's corpus. In *Proceedings of the Tenth International Conference on Language Resources and Evaluation (LREC'16)*, pages 1808-1812. European Language Resources Association (ELRA), May 2016. (Cite on page 51)

A.-K. Al-Tamimi, M. Jaradat, N. Aljarrah, and S. Ghanim. Aari: Automatic arabic readability index. *International Arab Journal of Information Technology*, 11:370-378, 07 2014. (Cited on pages 19, 32, 33 and 51)

A. Al-Wabil, E. Meldah, A. Al-Suwaidan, and A. AlZahrani. Designing educational games for children with specific learning difficulties: Insights from involving children and practitioners. pages 195 - 198, 10 2010. doi : 10.1109/ICCGI.2010.43. (Cite en page 9)

S. Almujaiwel. *Free/open KACSTAC and its processing tools : Lexical resources for Arabic lexicogrammatical microstructures based on collocational indicators*, pages 153-170. 01 2016. ISBN (10) : 1-4438-8513-4. (Cite on page 19)

A. Alotaibi. The effect of font size and type on reading performance with Arabic words in normally sighted and simulated cataract subjects. *Clinical and experimental optometry : journal of the Australian Optometrical Association*, 90:203-6, 05 2007. doi : 10.1111/j. 1444-0938.2007.00123.x. (Cite on page 10)

S. Alotaibi, M. Alyahya, H. Al-Khalifa, S. Alageel, and N. Abanmy. Readability of arabic medicine information leaflets: A machine learning approach. *Procedia Computer Science*, 82:122 - 126, 2016. ISSN 1877-0509. doi : https://doi.org/10.1016/j.procs. 2016.04.017. 4th Symposium on Data Mining Applications, SDMA2016, 30 March 2016, Riyadh, Saudi Arabia (Cite on page 35)

M. Althobaiti, U. Kruschwitz, and M. Poesio. Aranlp : a java-based library for the processing of arabic text. In *Proceedings of the Ninth International Conference on Language Resources and Evaluation (LREC'14)*, pages 4134-4138, Reykjavik, Iceland, May 2014. European Language Resources Association (ELRA). URL http://www. lrec-conf.org/proceedings/lrec2014/pdf/621_Paper.pdf. (Cite on page 71)

J. Anderson. Lix and rix: Variations on a little-known readability index. *Journal of Reading,* 26(6) :490-496, 1983. ISSN 00224103. URL http://www.jstor.org/stable/ 40031755. (Cite on page 16)

E. k. Anoual and A. Lakhouaja. Arabic learning disabilities in public primary schools : The case of east side of morocco. pages 1-5, 12 2015. doi : 10.1109/ICTA.2015.7426906. (Cite en page 33)

N. Bhargava, G. Sharma, R. Bhargava, and M. Mathuria. Decision tree analysis on j48 algorithm for data mining. volume 3, 2013. (Cite on page 26)

C. Biemann, G. Heyer, U. Quasthoff, and M. Richter. The leipzig corpora collectionmonolingual corpora of standard size. *Proceedings of Corpus Linguistic*, 2007, 2007. (Quoted on page 40)

W. Black, S. Elkateb, H. Rodriguez, M. Alkhalifa, P. Vossen, A. Pease, and C. Fellbaum. Introducing the arabic wordnet project. In *Proceedings of the third international Word- Net conference*, pages 295-300. Citeseer, 2006. (Cited on page 106)

H. Bobzin. On the frequency of verbs in modern newspaper Arabic. 1983 (Quoted on page 41)

J. R. Bormuth. The cloze readability procedure. *Elementary English*, 45(4) :429-436, 1968. ISSN 00135968. URL http://www.jstor.org/stable/41386340. (Quoted on page 16)

N. Boudad, R. Faizi, R. Oulad Haj Thami, and R. Chiheb. Sentiment analysis in arabic : A review of the literature. *Ain Shams Engineering Journal*, 9(4) :2479 - 2490, 2018. ISSN 2090-4479. doi : https://doi.org/10.1016/j.asej.2017.04.007. URL http://www. sciencedirect.com/science/article/pii/S2090447917300862. (Cite on page 5)

M. Boudchiche and A. Mazroui. A hybrid approach for Arabic lemmatization. *International Journal of Speech Technology*, 22(3) :563-573, Sept. 2019. ISSN 1572-8110. doi : 10.1007/s10772-018-9528-3. (Cite on page 45)

L. Breiman. Random Forests. *Machine Learning*, 45(1) :5-32, Oct. 2001. ISSN 1573-0565. doi : 10.1023/A:1010933404324. URL https://doi.org/10.1023/A:1010933404324. (Cite on page 26)

A.-T. Brustad, Al-Batal. *Al-Kitaab fii Tacallum alArabiya, A Textbook for Beginning Arabic: Part Two*. Georgetown University Press, 2007. (Quoted on page 29)

T. Buckwalter and D. Parkinson. *A frequency dictionary of Arabic: Core vocabulary for learners*. Routledge, 2014. (Cited on pages 28 and 42)

V. Cavalli-Sforza, M. El Mezouar, and H. Saddiki. Matching an Arabic text to a learners' curriculum. page 10, 2014. (Cited on pages xi, 29, 32, 33 and 96)

J. S. Chall and E. Dale. *Readability revisited: The new Dale-Chal readability formula*. Brookline Books, 1995 (Cited on page 17).

N. Chawla, K. Bowyer, L. Hall, and W. Kegelmeyer. Smote: Synthetic minority oversampling technique. *J. Artif. Intell. Res. (JAIR)*, 16:321-357, 06 2002. doi : 10.1613/ jair.953 (Cite on page 88)

C. J. Chen, M. W. Y. Keong, C. S. Teh, and K. M. Chuah. Web text reading: what satisfy both dyslexic and normal learners? *Journal of Computers in Education*, 3(1) : 47-58, Mar. 2016. ISSN 2197-9995. doi : 10.1007/s40692-015-0046-x. URL https: //doi.org/10.1007/s40692-015-0046-x. (Quoted on page 9)

A. Chennoufi and A. Mazroui. Impact of morphological analysis and a large training corpus on the performances of Arabic diacritization. *International Journal of Speech Technology*, 19(2) :269-280, June 2016. ISSN 1572-8110. doi : 10.1007/s10772-015-9313-5. URL https://doi.org/10.1007/s10772-015-9313-5. (Cite on page 42)

J. L. D. Clark and R. T. Clifford. The fsi/ilr/actfl proficiency scales and testing techniques: Development, current status, and needed research. *Studies in Second Language Acquisition*, 10(2) :129-147, 1988. doi : 10.1017/S0272263100007270 (Cite en page 27)

K. Collins-Thompson and J. Callan. Information retrieval for language tutoring: An overview of the reap project. pages 544-545, 01 2004. doi : 10.1145/1008992.1009112. (Cite on page 26)

M. Cronin, S. O'Hanlon, and M. O'Connor. Readability level of patient information leaflets for older people. *Irish Journal of Medical Science*, 180(1) :139-142, Mar. 2011. ISSN 1863-4362. doi : 10.1007/s11845-010-0624-x. URL https://doi.org/10.1007/ s11845-010-0624-x. (Quoted on page 34)

5. A. Crossley, S. Skalicky, M. Dascalu, D. S. McNamara, and K. Kyle. Predicting text comprehension, processing, and familiarity in adult readers: New approaches to readability formulas. *Discourse Processes*, 54(5-6) :340-359, 2017. doi : 10.1080/0163853X.2017.1296264. (Cite on page 30)

W. Daelemans, J. Zavrel, K. Sloot, and A. Van den Bosch. Timbl: Tilburg memory-based learner. 02 2004. (Cited on page 29)

E. Dale and J. S. Chall. A formula for predicting readability. *Educational Research Bulletin,* 27(1) :11-28, 1948. ISSN 15554023. URL http://www.jstor.org/stable/ 1473169. (Cited on pages 17 and 25)

L. Daraz, A. Morrow, O. Ponce, W. Farah, A. Katabi, M. Seisa, R. Benkhadra, M. Al- sawas, P. Larry, and M. Murad. Readability of online health information: A metanarrative systematic review. *American Journal of Medical Quality*, 33:106286061775163, 01 2018. doi: 10.1177/1062860617751639. (Cite on page 35)

N. Daud, H. Hassan, and N. Aziz. A corpus-based readability formula for estimation of arabic texts reading difficulty. 2013. (Cite on page 19)

M. Davies and D. Gardner. *A frequency dictionary of contemporary American English: Word sketches, collocates and thematic lists*. Routledge, 2013. (Quoted on page 39)

B. Dawood. The relationship between readability and selected language variables. 1977 (Cited on page 18)

P. Di tore, S. Di Tore, G. Mangione, and L. Ludovico. *MADRIGALE: A Multimedia Application for Dyslexia and Reading Improvement GAmifying Learning Experience*. 09 2014. ISBN 978-1-4799-6386-7. doi : 10.1109/INCoS.2014.48. (Cite on page 9)

M. Diab. Second generation amira tools for arabic processing : Fast and robust tokeniza- tion, pos tagging, and base phrase chunking. 01 2009. (Cited on page 44)

M. Edmunds, R. Barry, and A. Denniston. Readability assessment of online ophthalmic patient information. *JAMA ophthalmology*, 131, 10 2013. doi : 10.1001/jamaophthalmol. 2013.5521.

(Cite on page 35)
M. EL-Haj and P. Rayson. Osman - a novel arabic readability metric. 05 2016. (Cited on pages 21, 32 and 33)
A. El Kah. Computer-assisted learning language for learning disabilities in the Arabic language: Diagnosis, training and assistance, 2019. (Cite on page 10)
A. El Kah and A. Lakhouaja. Developing effective educative games for Arabic children primarily dyslexics. *Education and Information Technologies*, 23(6) :2911-2930, Nov. 2018. ISSN 1573-7608. doi : 10.1007/s10639-018-9750-2. URL https://doi.org/10. 1007/s10639-018-9750-2. (Cite on page 9)
A. El Kah, I. Zeroual, and A. Lakhouaja. Application of arabic language processing in language learning. In *Proceedings of the 2Nd International Conference on Big Data, Cloud and Applications,* BDCA'17, pages 35:1-35:6, New York, NY, USA, 2017. ACM. ISBN 978-1-4503-4852-2. doi: 10.1145/3090354.3090390. (Cite on page 58)
M. Eros. *Al-Kitaab fii Ta'al lum Al-'Arabiyya with DVDs: A Textbook for Beginning Arabic, Part One*, volume 59. Middle East Institute, 2005. (Quoted on page 29)
R. Evans, C. Orasan, and I. Dornescu. An evaluation of syntactic simplification rules for people with autism. In *Proceedings of the 3rd Workshop on Predicting and Improving Text Readability for Target Reader Populations (PITR*), pages 131-140, Gothenburg, Sweden, Apr. 2014. Association for Computational Linguistics. doi : 10.3115/v1/W14-1215. URL https://www.aclweb.org/anthology/W14-1215. (Cite on page 103)
L. Feng, N. Elhadad, and M. Huenerfauth. Cognitively motivated features for readability assessment. pages 229-237, 01 2009. doi : 10.3115/1609067.1609092. (Cite en page 33)
L. Feng, M. Jansche, M. Huenerfauth, and N. Elhadad. A comparison of features for automatic readability assessment. In *Proceedings of the 23rd International Conference on Computational Linguistics : Posters*, COLING '10, page 276-284, USA, 2010. Association for Computational Linguistics (Cite on pages 22 and 30).
R. Flesch. A new readability yardstick. *Journal of Applied Psychology*, 32(3) :221, June 1948. ISSN 1939-1854 (Electronic), 0021-9010 (Print). doi : 10.1037/h0057532 (Cite on page 15)
J. Forsyth. Automatic Readability Detection for Modern Standard Arabic, 2014. (Cited on pages xi, 28, 29, 32, 33, 69, 73 and 90)
T. Francois and E. Miltsakaki. Do NLP and machine learning improve traditional readability formulas? In *Proceedings of the First Workshop on Predicting and Improving Text Readability for target reader populations*, pages 49-57, Montreal, Canada, June 2012. Association for Computational Linguistics. URL https://www.aclweb.org/anthology/ W12-2207. (Cite on page 27)
N. Gala, A. Tack, L. Javourey-Drevet, T. Francois, and J. C. Ziegler. Alector : A parallel corpus of simplified French texts with alignments of misreadings by poor and dyslexic readers. In *Proceedings of the 12th Language Resources and Evaluation Conference*, pages 1353-1361, Marseille, France, May 2020. European Language Resources Association. ISBN 979-10-95546-34-4. URL https://www.aclweb.org/anthology/2020. lrec-1.169. (Cite on page 103)
D. Gemoets, G. Rosemblat, T. Tse, and R. Logan. Assessing readability of consumer health information: An exploratory study. *Studies in health technology and informatics*, 107:869-73, 02 2004. doi : 10.3233/978-1-60750-949-3-869. (Cite en page 34)
K. Ghani, A. Noh, and N. Mohd Rahimi. Linguistic features for development of arabic text readability formula in malaysia: A preliminary study. *Middle - East Journal of Scientific Research*, 19:319-331, 01 2014. doi : 10.5829/idosi.mejsr.2014.19.3.13597. (Cite on page 20)

W. S. Gray and B. E. Leary. What makes a book readable. 1935 (Quoted on page 1)

R. Gunning. The fog index after twenty years. *Journal of Business Communication*, 6 (2) :3-13, 1969. doi : 10.1177/002194366900600202. URL https://doi.org/10.1177/002194366900600202. (Cite on page 17)

N. Habash, O. Rambow, and R. Roth. Mada+tokan : A toolkit for arabic tokenization, diacritization, morphological disambiguation, pos tagging, stemming and lemmatiza- tion. *Proceedings of the 2nd International Conference on Arabic Language Resources and Tools (MEDAR)*, 01 2009. (Cited on pages 29 and 44)

N. Habash, B. Mohit, O. Obeid, K. Oflazer, N. Tomeh, and W. Zaghouani. Qalb : Qatar arabic language bank. In *Proceedings of Qatar Annual Research Conference (ARC- 2013)*, Doha, Qatar, 2013. (Cite on page 52)

M. Hall. Correlation-based feature selection for machine learning. *Department of Computer Science*, 19, 06 2000. (Cited on page 86)

M. Heilman, K. Collins-Thompson, J. Callan, and M. Eskenazi. Classroom success of an intelligent tutoring system for lexical practice and reading comprehension. volume 2, 01 2006. (Cite on page 26)

A. C. Hickson. Readability and quality of online information regarding the hearing disorder "auditory processing disorder", 2020. (Quoted on page 33)

J. E. Hoard, R. Wojcik, and K. Holzhauser. *An Automated Grammar and Style Checker for Writers of Simplified English*, pages 278-296. Springer Netherlands, Dordrecht, 1992. ISBN 978-94-011-2854-4. doi: 10.1007/978-94-011-2854-4_19. URL https: //doi.org/10.1007/978-94-011-2854-4_19 (Cited on page 104).

J. E. Hofman and M. Habib-Allah. The cloze technique in Arabic : Words or semantic units ? *Journal of Psycholinguistic Research*, 11(4) :275-282, July 1982. ISSN 15736555. doi : 10.1007/BF01067582. URL https://doi.org/10.1007/BF01067582. (Cite on page 18)

G. Holmes, A. Donkin, and I. Witten. Weka: A machine learning workbench. pages 357 - 361, 01 1994. ISBN 0-7803-2404-8. doi : 10.1109/ANZIIS.1994.396988 (Cite on page 31)

G. Husseinali. Who is studying Arabic and why? A survey of Arabic students' orientations at a major university. *Foreign Language Annals*, 39:395 - 412, 12 2008. doi : 10.1111/ j.1944-9720.2006.tb02896.x. (Cite on page 10)

M. Junczys-Dowmunt, T. Dwojak, and H. Hoang. Is neural machine translation ready for deployment? a case study on 30 translation directions. 01 2016. (Cite on page 105)

D. Kauchak and G. Leroy. A web-based medical text simplification tool. 01 2020. doi : 10.24251/HICSS.2020.458 (Cite on page 104)

J. P. Kincaid, R. P. Fishburne Jr, R. L. Rogers, and B. S. Chissom. Derivation of new readability formulas (automated readability index, fog count and flesch reading ease formula) for navy enlisted personnel. 1975 (Cited on page 16).

R. E. Korf. Linear-space best-first search. *Artificial Intel ligence*, 62(1) :41 - 78, 1993. ISSN 0004-3702. doi : https://doi.org/10.1016/0004-3702(93)90045-D. URL http://www.sciencedirect.com/science/article/pii/000437029390045D. (Cite on page 86)

D. E. Kouloughli. *Lexique fondamental de l'arabe standard moderne*. Editions L'Harmat- tan, 1991 (quoted on page 41).

J. M. Landau. *A word count of modern Arabic prose*. Number 17. American Council of Learned Societies, 1971 (Quoted on page 41).

B. Laufer. The development of passive and active vocabulary in a second language: Same or different? *Applied Linguistics*, 19, 06 1998. doi : 10.1093/applin/19.2.255 (Cite en page 40)

J. B. Lieberman. *Types of Typefaces and how to Recognize Them.* Sterling Publishing Company, 1967 (Quoted on page 8).

A. C. Liu. The effect of oversampling and undersampling on classifying imbalanced text datasets. *The University of Texas at Austin*, 2004. (Cited on page 88)

D. Lonsdale and Y. Le Bras. *A frequency dictionary of French: Core vocabulary for learners*. Routledge, 2009. (Quoted on page 39)

D. Looney and N. Lusin. Enrollments in languages other than english in united states institutions of higher education, summer 2016 and fall 2016: Preliminary report. In *Modern Language Association*. ERIC, 2018. (Cite on page 11)

M. B. Marr. An analysis of text variables in three current reading diagnostic tests. 1982 (Cited on page 16)

L. Martin, A. Fan, E. De la Clergerie, A. Bordes, and B. Sagot. Multilingual unsupervised sentence simplification. 05 2020. (Quoted on page 104)

A. Masrai and J. Milton. How many words do you need to speak Arabic? an Arabic vocabulary size test. *Language Learning Journal,* pages 1-18, 01 2017. doi : 10.1080/09571736.2016.1258720. (Cite on page 40)

M. M. McClelland, A. C. Acock, and F. J. Morrison. The impact of kindergarten learning-related skills on academic trajectories at the end of elementary school. *Early Childhood Research Quarterly*, 21(4) :471 - 490, 2006. ISSN 0885-2006. doi : https://doi.org/10.1016/j.ecresq.2006.09.003. (Quoted on page 58)

N. H. McLaughlin. SMOG grading: A new readability formula. *Journal of Reading*, 12 (8) :639-646, 1969 (Cite on page 17)

D. Meyer and R. Schvaneveldt. Facilitation in recognizing pairs of words: Evidence of a dependence between retrieval operations. *Journal of experimental psychology*, 90: 227-34, 11 1971. doi : 10.1037/h0031564 (Cite on page 31)

A. Miniukovich, A. De Angeli, S. Sulpizio, and P. Venuti. Design guidelines for web readability. pages 285-296, 06 2017. doi : 10.1145/3064663.3064711. (Cite on page 9)

O. Mohammadi and S. H. Khasteh. Text as environment: A deep reinforcement learning text readability assessment model. 12 2019. (Cite on page 27)

A. Mucherino, P. J. Papajorgji, and P. M. Pardalos. *k-Nearest Neighbor Classification*, pages 83-106. Springer New York, New York, NY, 2009. ISBN 978-0387-88615-2. doi : 10.1007/978-0-387-88615-2_4. URL https://doi.org/10.1007/ 978-0-387-88615-2_4. (Quoted on page 26)

S. Mustafa. Word stemming for arabic information retrieval: The case for light stemming. 21:123-144, 01 2012. (Cite on page 55)

T. Mustonen, M. Olkkonen, and J. Hakkinen. Examining mobile phone text legibility while walking. In *CHI '04 Extended Abstracts on Human Factors in Computing Systems*, CHI EA '04, page 1243-1246, New York, NY, USA, 2004. Association for Computing Machinery. ISBN 1581137036. doi : 10.1145/985921.986034. URL https://doi.org/ 10.1145/985921.986034. (Quoted on page 2)

N. Nassiri, A. Lakhouaja, and V. Cavalli-Sforza. Modern standard arabic readability prediction. In A. Lachkar, K. Bouzoubaa, A. Mazroui, A. Hamdani, and A. Lekhouaja, editors, *Arabic Language Processing: From Theory to Practice,* pages 120-133, Cham, 2018a. Springer International Publishing. ISBN 978-3-319-73500-9 (Cited on page 71).

N. Nassiri, A. Lakhouaja, and V. Cavalli-Sforza. Arabic readability assessment for foreign language learners. In M. Silberztein, F. Atigui, E. Kornyshova, E. Metais, and F. Me- ziane, editors, *Natural Language Processing and Information Systems*, pages 480-488, Cham,

2018b. Springer International Publishing. ISBN 978-3-319-91947-8. (Quoted on page 79)

N. Nassiri, V. Cavalli-Sforza, and A. Lakhouaja. Mosar: Modern standard Arabic readability corpus for l1 learners. In *Proceedings of the 4th International Conference on Big Data and Internet of Things*, BDIoT'19, New York, NY, USA, 2019. Association for Computing Machinery. ISBN 9781450372404. doi : 10.1145/3372938.3372961. (Cite on page 51)

J. Ohene-Djan and M. Gorle. An adaptive function for hypermedia-based advanced learning technology. page 464, 08 2003. doi : 10.1109/ICALT.2003.1215187 (Cite en page 9)

A. Pasha, M. Al-Badrashiny, M. Diab, A. El Kholy, R. Eskander, N. Habash, M. Pooleery, O. Rambow, and R. Roth. Madamira: A fast, comprehensive tool for morphological analysis and disambiguation of arabic. In *Proceedings of the Ninth International Conference on Language Resources and Evaluation (LREC'14)*, pages 1094-1101. European Language Resources Association (ELRA), May 2014. (Cite on page 44)

L. Rello, R. Baeza-Yates, S. Bott, and H. Saggion. Simplify or help ? text simplification strategies for people with dyslexia. In *Proceedings of the 10th International CrossDisciplinary Conference on Web Accessibility*, W4A '13, New York, NY, USA, 2013a. Association for Computing Machinery. ISBN 9781450318440. doi : 10.1145/2461121. 2461126. URL https://doi.org/10.1145/2461121.2461126. (Cited on page 103)

L. Rello, R. Baeza-Yates, L. Dempere-Marco, and H. Saggion. Frequent words improve readability and short words improve understandability for people with dyslexia. In *Human-Computer Interaction - INTERACT 2013*, pages 203-219. Springer Berlin Heidelberg, 2013b. ISBN 978-3-642-40498-6 (Quoted on page 34)

M. Reqqass, A. Lakhouaja, and M. Bebah. "alkhalildws": An arabic dictionary writing system rich in lexical resources. In K. Smaili, editor, *Arabic Language Processing: From Theory to Practice,* pages 237-250, Cham, 2019. Springer International Publishing. ISBN 978-3-030-32959-4. (Quoted on page 12)

H. Saddiki, K. Bouzoubaa, and V. Cavalli-Sforza. Text readability for arabic as a foreign language. pages 1-8, 11 2015. doi : 10.1109/AICCSA.2015.7507232. (Cite in pages xi, 29, 30, 32, 33, 73 and 90)

H. Saddiki, N. Habash, V. Cavalli-Sforza, and M. Al Khalil. Feature optimization for predicting readability of Arabic L1 and L2. In *Proceedings of the 5th Workshop on Natural Language Processing Techniques for Educational Applications*, pages 20-29, Melbourne, Australia, July 2018. Association for Computational Linguistics. doi: 10. 18653/v1/W18-3703. URL https://www.aclweb.org/anthology/W18-3703. (Cited on pages 30, 32 and 33)

S. F. J. Schonell and I. G. Meddleton. *A study of the oral vocabulary of adults*. Queensland UP, 1956 (Cited on pages 39 and 40).

R. Senter and E. A. Smith. Automated readability index. 1967 (Quoted on page 17)

R. Shedlosky-Shoemaker, A. Sturm, M. Saleem, and K. Kelly. Tools for assessing readability and quality of health-related web sites. *Journal of Genetic Counseling*, 18:49-59, 02 2009. doi : 10.1007/s10897-008-9181-0. (Cite on page 34)

G. Silva. A frequency dictionary of portuguese : Core vocabulary for learners by davies, mark and ana maria raposo preto-bay. *Modern Language Journal - MOD LANG J*, 93: 322-323, 06 2009. doi : 10.1111/j.1540-4781.2009.00870_20.x. (Cited on page 39)

S. L. SMITH. Letter size and legibility. *Human Factors*, 21(6) :661-670, 1979. doi : 10.1177/001872087912210604. (Cite on page 2)

M. Sprengling. The basic word list of the arabic daily newspaper. moshe brill , d. neustadt , p. schusser. *Journal of Near Eastern Studies*, 2(3) :205-207, 1943. doi : 10.1086/370679. URL https://doi.org/10.1086/370679. (Cited on page 41)

A. Stolcke. Srilm - an extensible language modeling toolkit. *Proceedings of the 7th International Conference on Spoken Language Processing (ICSLP 2002)*, 2, 07 2004. (Cite on page 31)

t. JiU. JaU >li ^aA2U-(*UNI J3 ^311 3Ш ^Vl ^i) UlJfcVI 6^211 <U^V1 oh>11, 1942 (Quoted on page 41).

6J4ft <^ jjlл .^jdl Aiill ^i 4*3UU olз>11 ^ba ^i ^ic :Д^.y*Л Aiill ^i 4^11 ol3ji-11 1979 (Quoted on page 41).

E. L. Thorndike. *The teacher's word book*. Teacher's College, Columbia University, 1921 (Quoted on page 14).

W. Tracy. *Letters of credit: a view of type design.* Boston: David R, 1986 (Cited on page 8).

R. A. Tu'aymah. *al-marja'fi ta'lim al-lughah li natiqin bi lughah ukhra*. Macca: Ummu al-Qurra University, 1986 (Quoted on page 40).

S. Vajjala and D. Meurers. On improving the accuracy of readability classification using insights from second language acquisition. In *Proceedings of the Seventh Workshop on Building Educational Applications Using NLP*, NAACL HLT '12, page 163-173, USA, 2012. Association for Computational Linguistics (Cite on page 27).

E. B. Welles. Foreign language enrollments in united states institutions of higher education, fall 2002. *Profession*, pages 128-153, 2004. ISSN 07406959, 19381522. URL http://www.jstor.org/stable/25595784. (Cite on page 11)

S. Wubben, A. van den Bosch, and E. Krahmer. Sentence simplification by monolingual machine translation. In *Proceedings of the 50th Annual Meeting of the Association for Computational Linguistics (Volume 1: Long Papers)*, pages 1015-1024, Jeju Island, Korea, July 2012. Association for Computational Linguistics. URL https://www.aclweb.org/anthology/P12-1107. (Cite on page 104)

W. Xu, C. Callison-Burch, and C. Napoles. Problems in current text simplification research: New data can help. *Transactions of the Association for Computational Linguistics*, 3:283-297, 2015. doi: 10.1162/tacl_a_00139. URL https://www.aclweb. org/anthology/Q15-1021. (Cite on page 103)

T. Zerrouki and A. Balla. Tashkeela: Novel corpus of Arabic vocalized texts, data for auto-diacritization systems. *Data in Brief*, 11:147-151, 2017. ISSN 2352-3409. doi: 10.1016/j.dib.2017.01.011. (Cite on page 42)

H. Zhao and J. Yu. A modified smo algorithm for svm regression and its application in quality prediction of hp-ldpe. In L. Wang, K. Chen, and Y. S. Ong, editors, *Advances in Natural Computation*, pages 630-639, Berlin, Heidelberg, 2005. Springer Berlin Heidelberg. ISBN 978-3-540-31853-8. (Quoted on page 26)

M. Ziemski, M. Junczys-Dowmunt, and B. Pouliquen. The United Nations parallel corpus v1.0. In *Proceedings of the Tenth International Conference on Language Resources and Evaluation (LREC'16),* pages 3530-3534, Portoroz, Slovenia, May 2016. European Language Resources Association (ELRA). URL https://www.aclweb.org/anthology/ L16-1561. (Cite on page 21)

G. K. Zipf. *Human behavior and the principle of least effort.* addison-wesley press, 1949. (Cite on page 15)

MIX
Papier aus verantwortungsvollen Quellen
Paper from responsible sources
FSC® C105338

FSC
www.fsc.org

Printed by Books on Demand GmbH, Norderstedt / Germany